Test Your IQ

Test Your IQ

Eamonn Butler and
Madsen Pirie

Pan Books London, Sydney and Auckland

First published 1983 by Pan Books Ltd,
Cavaye Place. London SW10 9PG
20 19 18 17
© Eamonn Butler and Madsen Pirie 1983
ISBN 0 330 26712 4

Printed and bound in Great Britain by
Richard Clay Ltd, Bungay, Suffolk

Contents

Acknowledgements

Thanks are due to several Mensans for their help. Kevin Browne and Carole Clarke gave valuable and much appreciated assistance. Special thanks are also owed to Harold Gale, Mensa's Executive Director, and Victor Serebriakoff, the President of Mensa. Finally we must thank all of the Mensans who participated in our tests; readers interested in joining them are invited to write for details to Mensa, Freepost, Wolverhampton.

Dr. Eamonn Butler
Dr. Madsen Pirie

Introduction

There may be one of two paradoxical reasons why a concept is rarely mentioned in the pages of the philosophy and literature of the last three millennia. One is that the concept is so familiar and mundane that no author deems it worthy of note. The other is that it is so abstruse and elusive that it cannot readily be put into words. The concept of intelligence, one of the most underwritten ideas in human speculation over the ages, seems to have been suppressed by the second explanation, for it is only in this century that we have had a clear understanding of the nature of intelligence and have been able to isolate it from related human abilities and similar concepts.

The Greek philosophers and scientists of the ancient world were surprisingly advanced in most of their writings, especially those concerning the nature of the physical world, a world which could be observed and tested. But their views on metaphysics and psychology suffered because of their failure to recognise the important influence of language upon thought. When they speculated about human mental ability, the Greeks were yoked with the word *nous* – a portmanteau word which covered the concepts of soul, mind, spirit and thinking, as well as that of mental ability. It is a tribute to the brilliance of Plato and Aristotle that they were able to unravel these confused ideas at all, but not surprising that their attempts are imperfect.

Plato was the first to begin the discussion on intelligence with his tripartite division of the *nous*. Everyone, he said, has an appetitive part to him, an impulsive side to his nature. In addition, there is the element of thought, or reasoning. And there is another element between them, which takes order from the reasoning side and curbs the excesses of the impulsive side. In his *Republic*, one of the earliest attempts to build a utopia upon a mistaken notion of human nature, this tripartite division of human nature is reflected in a tripartite division of human classes in Plato's ideal state.

In the *Phaedrus* also, Plato gives us a vivid analogy to demonstrate his division of human nature. Here, the reason or intellect is cast in the role of a charioteer, controlling two horses. One, analogous to the appetitive element, tends to leap wildly forward, causing all kinds of trouble for the other horse, which is constrained by its noble breeding. But the rational element in the shape of the charioteer brings them under control, each as necessary, until he has mastery over them. So in this analogy, Plato has suggested that the noble and ignoble parts provide the motive forces in an individual, while reason gives them their direction.

This is still far from the modern notion of intelligence, but Plato does offer some further remarks on the balance of environment and heredity in personal abilities that are strikingly modern. In the *Republic*, he makes it quite plain that he thinks human differences stem principally from inheritance. Thus he suggests that it is relatively easy to divide people into different classes; and he recommends that to avoid envy between the classes, people should be told that 'the god who fashioned you mixed gold in the composition of those among you who are fit to rule, so that they are of the most precious quality; and he put silver in the auxiliaries, and iron and brass in the farmers and workmen'. But things are not quite that simple. Modern genetics recognises the concept of *regression towards the mean* – that intelligent parents have children who tend to be less intelligent, while dull parents have children who tend to be brighter. Plato recognises this phenomenon when he continues:

> Now, since you are all of one stock, although your children will generally be like their parents, sometimes a golden parent may have a silver child or a silver parent a golden one, and so on with all the other combinations. So the first and chief injunction laid by heaven upon the rulers is that among all the things of which they must show themselves to be good guardians, there is none that needs to be so carefully watched as the mixture of metals in their children. If a child of their own is born with an alloy of brass or iron, they must, without the smallest pity, assign him the station proper to his nature and thrust him out among the craftsmen or the farmers.

The ability of their children is still a subject which causes the greatest concern to parents, although its consequences are perhaps less brutal today than in Plato's utopia.

The theory of intelligence took another step forward with Plato's disciple Aristotle, who extracted cognition from perception. His idea of mental functions separated the nutritive, the perceptive, the motive and the intelligence. To him, the intelligence ordered outside objects, just as the senses perceived them. Intelligence was therefore passive and, unlike the other parts of the mind, was not shared by plants or animals. Aristotle thought that the use of this intelligence in a life of contemplation was the highest achievement of man, and he was sufficiently wealthy to pursue this course himself.

The thinkers of the Roman period made little further contribution to this line of reasoning, although they seem to have had a more practical understanding of individual differences of intellect than is evident in Greek writing. Cicero, an orator who succeeded in devising a mostly original philosophical system of his own, drew on the Greek concept of intellectual and cognitive powers to coin the term *intelligentsia*, which is with us today. Quintilian in AD 70 drew attention to the diversity of abilities within schoolchildren, a spread of talent that was as varied as the differences in bodily features. Virgil and the other poets of the age preserved the division between intellect and spirit or appetite.

But from the birth of Christ to the Renaissance, one has to look hard to find much original thought on the subject. St Augustine characteristically adopted an Aristotelian view. Aquinas argued that the intellect was not physical, but outside space and time and therefore infinite in a sense. He also believed that

> The power of understanding does not consist in the activity of corporeal organs and so, although the natures that it connaturally knows cannot exist except in individual matter, it knows them not merely as they are in such matter, but as made abstract by the operation of the mind. Thus by understanding we can know things universally, something that is beyond the scope of the senses.

The power of abstraction and the 'eduction of relations and correlates' that are principles of the modern view of intelligence can thus be traced back to the thirteenth century.

An engaging but very different view of human intellectual abilities arises in the work *De l'Ésprit des Lois*, written by Baron de Montesquieu in 1748. He suggested that the physical environment was of great importance in determining the characteristics of peoples, and that these differences were due to bodily differences. Heat, he tells us, expands the ends of the nerve fibres, making people from hot climates sensitive, but lazy and timid. Those from cold climates are, contrariwise, tough and active: an early explanation of how the working of the mind can be reduced to physical, empirical causes.

It is in this tradition that the modern approach to intelligence and intelligence testing began. Convinced Darwinists such as Herbert Spencer supposed that intelligence was a heritable characteristic which helped explain the relative success or failure of different groups in the human population. Darwin's own cousin, Francis Galton, also believed that intelligence was inherited, and that it should be possible therefore to raise the average intelligence level in a population by finding out which members were dull and discouraging them from having children. (In this, he seems to have known less about the laws of inheritance than did Plato in the allegory of the metals, for the children of dull parents will tend to be brighter than them.)

The first thought was that intelligence was related to some physical characteristic and could thus be precisely measured. Galton and others embarked upon countless laboratory tests, measuring head sizes, brain weights and even the reaction time to flashing lights or a tap on the kneecap. But no physiological test then devised could distinguish between the brightest student and a mental defective.

It seems rather obvious to us now that if we are to measure mental abilities, a mental test is the right tool. But we had to wait until 1905 before the French psychologist Alfred Binet drew up the first. The French ministry of public teaching established a working party at this time, in an attempt to find out which school-students were unlikely to benefit much from the standard teaching methods because of their dullness, so that they could be given remedial courses which it was hoped would improve their abilities. Binet's test included thirty items which relied on an amount of general knowledge, but also measured reasoning and judgement. As modern intelligence tests go, it was not very good, containing too many knowledge requirements and not enough reasoning requirements, but scores related closely to children's success at school, and therefore it was given wide use by teachers.

The next major step was taken by Charles Spearman in England. He suggested that it should be possible to take the knowledge element out of mental tests. If there was in fact a general intellectual ability which enabled individuals to perform well on all kinds of problem – he referred to it by the letter g – then this could be tested quite simply. All that was necessary was to give large numbers of tests to large numbers of people and perform a statistical analysis to see whether those who performed well on one kind of test also tended to perform well on other kinds. And his researches confirmed this to be the case.

Subsequently, there were numerous academic exchanges between Spearman and L. L. Thurstone at the University of Chicago, who argued that there were in fact a number of related intellectual abilities which were lumped together in the Spearman test. Subsequent research by both scientists came to the conclusion which is largely unchanged today: people who are good on one general test tend to be good on another, although the same person can have rather different levels of skill at solving problems of different kinds, for example linguistic problems, number questions, memory or visual tasks.

Thus the concept of intelligence has changed little in the last half-century, although there has been a lively discussion about it. Radically different theories, such as those of Guilford and others, have been proposed; authors such as Leon Kamin accept the general value of intelligence tests (while pointing out that every test is only a rough guide to real abilities), but insist that mental ability is largely a product of environment, not inheritance. Jensen, Eysenck and others have sought for new physiological tests which correlate with mental test scores, and there have been neurological researches which attempt to discover exactly what it is in a person's body that makes him brighter or duller than others. But by and large, the model of intelligence and intelligence testing proposed by Spearman and Thurstone has proved its value and continues to survive.

General ability, special abilities and IQ tests

The common view of intelligence is that each person has a definite, unchanging degree of mental ability, and that this is objectively measured by intelligence tests and expressed as a single number, the intelligence quotient or IQ. But measuring mental ability is not like measuring the size of a room or counting up the number of pages in a book. On the contrary, we find that the same person will have different IQ scores if tested at different times; and, even more upsetting to the layman, we find that an individual often scores very differently on different kinds of intelligence test. This often shakes people's faith in any form of intelligence testing.

The scientist, however, is more familiar with this problem, and is unwilling to scrap intelligence testing because of it; for he recognises that IQ, like any physical measurement, is not the thing itself but merely an indicator of the thing.

Let us take the analogy of heat and temperature. If we leave a candle burning in an empty room, the temperature may rise very slightly. If we put the same candle under a cup of water, however, it might well reach the boil. In the same time period, the candle has put out the same amount of *heat*. But heat itself is rather difficult to measure, and we tend to use thermometers to measure a related thing, *temperature*. And in this case, we find that even though the candle has been burning for the same time, the temperature of the water has risen far more than the temperature of the empty room. A rise in temperature indicates that heat is flowing in to something: but how much heat has gone in is not the same as how much the temperature has risen, because the relationship between the two will depend upon the size and the nature of the object being heated. A thermometer is an *indicator* that heat is around, but does not measure it − only temperature. Likewise, the most we can say about IQ tests is that what they measure is only the ability to do them.

The thermometer analogy can be extended further. We use different kinds of thermometer to measure higher and lower temperatures. The very highest temperatures we measure using pyrometers, which detect the energy radiating from hot objects. At fairly high temperatures, such as those in a pottery kiln, we might use a thermocouple which detects electrical changes in metals caused by the rise in temperature. At more commonplace temperatures, we use mercury in glass thermometers. But at lower temperatures these are of little use because mercury freezes around $-37°C$, and in the Arctic and Antarctic alcohol thermometers which can be used down to $-115°C$ are necessary. But the remarkable thing is that the readings on these various kinds of thermometer are not consistent with one another. At the same temperature, two different kinds of thermometer will often give markedly different readings. It is not that one is 'right' and one is 'wrong' – they are indicators which behave differently, and it is up to us which one we care to choose. In the same way, two IQ tests can give different results, and whichever one we wish to choose depends on us.

Intelligence testers today accept that although there might be a sort of general intelligence g which affects a person's score on any kind of test, different people have different aptitudes, such as reasoning ability, visuo-spatial ability, verbal ability and numerical ability. A person who is good at visuo-spatial tasks will tend to excel on problems such as solving mazes, completing pictures, spotting which of a series of drawings is unlike others and so on. This is a special aptitude; but in addition, his general ability will make him reasonably good at other kinds of problem as well.

Most IQ tests attempt to mix together as many kinds of problem as possible in order to get at the general ability g and avoid giving excessive influence to any particular special aptitude. This is why they tend to be a mixture of number problems, word problems, picture questions and so on. What we are interested in is not the amount of a person's knowledge, nor his special abilities, but his general ability to see relationships between things, and to work out what new things fit in to those relationships. Take the following problem for example:

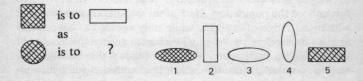

Here, we are told that there is a relationship between the two figures (although many IQ test questions do not even give this information and the person being tested has to work it out). When we examine it, we see that one object is black, the other white — there is one relationship, *opposite colour*. We see also that in order to convert the square into the oblong shown, we have to squash it flat as well as change its colour. Having established these two relations, we now have to apply them to the black circle and see which new figure would fit the blank space. Of course, it has to be the white figure like a squashed circle, figure 3. In solving this problem we have *educed a relation*, then used that relation to *educe a correlate*. And the ability to do those two things is just what Spearman in 1927 said should be tested by an intelligence test.

To construct a good test, there are a number of rules. The number of items should be fairly large, because the larger the number of items in a test, the more its results are free from chance effects and the more they agree with other tests. Similarly, we should choose items which tend to test general ability and do not have one special aptitude predominant. The value of a test item can in fact be judged by a statistical treatment called factor analysis. In a similar way, we can judge the difficulty of an item by examining the number of people who solve it, and a good test should have a spread of difficulty so that the scores on it clearly separate the bright from the dull — by adjusting the levels of difficulty, we can construct tests to be more accurate at higher or lower IQ scores.

If we take a test which conforms to these principles and give it to a very large number of people, we can compare their performance with the average. To calculate a person's IQ, we divide his score by the average score and multiply by 100. Thus average IQ would be 100, while scores above 100 indicate a higher than average IQ and scores below indicate a lower than average IQ. Large numbers of tests given to people over many years have left us with a very clear idea of how these scores are distributed throughout the population. Half of the population can be found within the range of 90–110, while only about 2% have scores above 130 or below 70. When IQ is charted against the number of individuals on each score, we see it follows the familiar bell-shaped 'normal' distribution which is so common when measuring any human characteristic. In fact there is a small bulge on the left-hand side of the curve, where physiological causes such as brain damage increase the numbers of very retarded people, but by and large the curve is symmetrical.

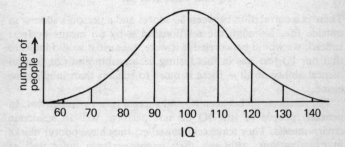

When a new test is drawn up, an individual's performance on it can be compared with his performance on other tests which may have been administered already to large groups of people, and in this way a new test can be standardised without our having to present it in such large numbers. But the higher or lower we go in IQ score, the fewer people there are whose scores we can compare, which is why IQ figures at the extremes have comparatively little meaning. As we get beyond 140, for example, we are standardising on so small a segment of the population that scores become less and less useful.

Even if a test is well drawn up, and eliminates the differences of special aptitudes, and even if it is designed with great care to be 'culture free' – that is, to be of an equal degree of difficulty to people whose educational or cultural backgrounds might be very different – there are factors in the individual which might still affect his performance.

It is not difficult to measure a piece of string; but depending on whether the string is wet or dry, different measurements might be obtained. Similarly with IQ scores, the result depends upon the condition of the person being tested. On one day a person might be a little tired; might be out of sorts; or if the test is important for some reason, might be suffering from examination nerves. On the other hand, the person being tested might be fit, refreshed and at the peak of form on the day. Factors such as these can all have a noticeable effect on the score, which is another reason why IQ results should be treated with caution.

IQ and success in life

There is a correlation between IQ scores and a person's success in outside life, although the relationship is by no means perfect. Indeed, we would be worried if it were, because it would indicate that our IQ test was in fact testing lifemanship and not general mental ability at all – there is more to success than intelligence alone.

The relationship between IQ and success is not symmetrical. In general, people of low IQ do not perform well in academic environments. They leave school earlier; they have poorer marks in examinations, although they might perform quite well at subjects such as athletics or woodwork, where less cognitive or thinking ability is required. By and large, they are not chosen for top posts, and are more likely to be manual workers than clerical workers or professional people. At the other end of the scale, high-IQ individuals may have plenty of ability to help them succeed, but lack the motivation or the luck to do it; it is easier for them to slip down the ladder of success than it is for the dull person to rise up it.

If we look at school life, we can see at once a strong relationship between IQ and academic performance, but IQ does not tell the whole story. In addition to straightforward ability, a school student will have to pick up background knowledge if he is to gain high marks. A high IQ is naturally an asset in this, but he will need a certain amount of motivation in order to improve his vocabulary, gain practice dealing with numbers, and absorb the finer points of his culture.

In fact there are a number of items which seem to affect performance at school, other than IQ. The first is obviously the range of subjects which a child is given. Children like different subjects for entirely personal reasons, not all of them linked to intelligence, and whether a child (or for that matter, a college student) really likes a subject is of crucial importance in determining his performance at it. Compounded with this is the view of his teachers, who may put an emphasis on some subjects rather than others; a child who is poor in verbal and numerical ability might be well compensated by good visuo-spatial and reasoning ability, but may perform poorly at a school specialising in 'traditional' subjects. On the other hand, he might perform extremely well at a science-oriented school.

The method of assessment is clearly another important factor. If a child is nervous when taking an IQ test because of its novel content, he might perform more poorly than he does in examinations about familiar subjects. If the schoolwork is tested without examinations, he might perform even better than his IQ score would suggest. Furthermore, success at school depends upon motivation. It is not uncommon to find a child who is more intelligent than his classmates but whose abilities do not show because the pace of the teaching is too slow for him. In this case, the child frequently interests himself in other things and performs very badly at school, despite his great ability. Personality differences also affect school performance. Extroverts tend to be interested in things outside the classroom, while introverts are more comfortable with their books. Some pupils see little point in struggling to succeed at school, while others put greater value on it. This all leads to the correlation being weakened.

Many of the same factors apply when we examine the performance of people in college and university life and compare it with their IQ scores. In general terms once again we can say that a university place in Britain is very unlikely to go to someone with an IQ less than 110, and 115 is about the lower limit for most students, the average tending to be about 125 or more. Again, the low-IQ individual does not have the mental ability to succeed in such academic pursuits, and however well motivated he is, it is difficult for him to get in; but the high-IQ individual, even though he has plenty of the required mental ability, very frequently does not enter or persist at university because he is unmotivated or lacks some necessary ingredient of character. While we can say that it would be almost impossible to earn a doctorate with an IQ of less than 130, for example, we cannot say that students of IQ 150 stand a better chance than those with an IQ of 140 – completing a doctorate is almost as much a question of stamina as of intelligence.

When we come to compare occupation with IQ, we find that the most intelligent people tend to be found in the higher professions, while the duller individuals tend to occupy semi-skilled and unskilled jobs. Once again, there is a spread of IQ range for each occupation, indicating that other factors are also at work, but a person's IQ is a good indicator of the status of job that he will finally hold. This effect is approximated in the following figure:

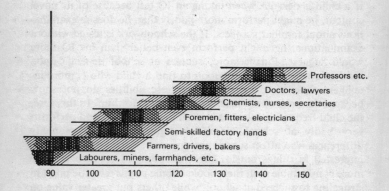

To be a professor, a top businessman, scientist or civil servant, it would be necessary to have an IQ of 140 or more, in the main; while it would be rare for anyone with an IQ much over 90 or 100 to opt to be a gardener or a factory hand in a monotonous job — although it is of course not unknown.

A great many IQ tests have been correlated against occupation and social position, and the overwhelming picture is of a relationship similar to that above. The army, which tests recruits routinely, provides a wealth of this material. Yerkes and others, on material from the First World War, showed that not only did IQ correlate with the occupations of recruits before they entered the army, but was closely linked to their eventual rank. The IQ distribution of officers peaked sharply at 135 on the army test (although that figure is not an IQ score) while sergeants tended to be more numerous at lower test scores. Corporals tended to be even lower when scored on the army test. Similarly, Second World War testing showed that over 90% of recruits with an IQ of 140 or more became commissioned officers, while less than half of those with a score of 110 succeeded.

One thing which this analysis does not enable us to do, however, is to work out who, of all the people who find themselves in the various professions, is likely to succeed. The analysis is a statistical one, which just points to the spread of sizeable groups of people across IQ and occupational groups, without saying anything about a particular individual. Also, the spread of IQ in any particular profession (say, of electricians) is likely to be only about 25–30 points anyway, and so the accuracy of our test may be insufficient to divide them confidently into those who will and those who will not succeed. But most importantly, it is a mixture of background, motivation and luck as well as intelligence which is needed for success.

The impact of age and sex on IQ

As might be expected, IQ scores are not constant over a person's lifetime. Children score much lower on IQ tests than do adults, and older people tend to score a little lower than people in the prime of life. When a child is very young, it is difficult to measure his intelligence with conventional IQ problems, but this becomes possible from the age of eight or so and we have a good idea of how intelligence scores increase from this age on. Typically, an individual's score increases almost linearly from age eight to the age of eighteen or twenty. From then on, it declines slowly over the individual's lifetime, thus:

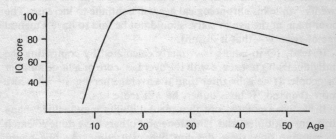

In individuals with higher IQ, the decline is not so marked as it is in the duller individuals, nor is it so rapid. But a person's IQ is roughly steady for most of his adult life.

The fact that intelligence test performance increases rapidly with age in children led Binet to take a very convenient measure to express the performance of any particular child with respect to the average. The ability of a child is obviously greater than average if he can solve problems that most children can answer only at a higher age. If a seven-year-old, for example, can answer problems which it normally takes ten-year-olds to solve, then his chronological age is seven, but his 'mental age' is ten — his mental performance is on a par with that of children of ten years of age. And similarly, if a ten-year-old child could not advance past problems that nine-year-olds could do, we would say he had a mental age of nine and a chronological age of ten. Thus when dealing with children we express the IQ as the ratio of mental age over chronological age, multiplied by 100. The IQ of the child taken as the first example would therefore be $10/7 \times 100$, or approximately 142. The IQ of the other child would be $9/10 \times 100$, or 90.

Some children, of course, are several years ahead of their fellows in mental ability, and so come out with very high IQ scores which settle down to lower levels in adult life. People who boast of particularly high IQs are often judging their remarks on the results of such tests at school, and their adult IQ might be much lower.

The principle of 'mental age divided by chronological age' is well known, and is responsible for some absurd misconceptions about IQ. If a man's IQ settles down at 100 at the age of twenty, he is about average: but we get into absurdity if we talk about 'mental age' at this level. For his 'mental age' will not rise above twenty, while his chronological age will continue to increase. The poor man, at the age of sixty, should not be said to have a mental age of twenty — that is absurd.

Instead, IQ in adults is properly calculated by comparing the individual's IQ test score with the average score of a large number of people. If he is brighter than the average person, he will score more than 100; if he is duller, he will score less.

It has been pointed out that mental ability may include many different aptitudes, and Thurstone and others have done research to examine how these develop over a lifetime. As one might expect, perceptual ability increases most rapidly, and reasoning and numerical skills develop after it. But verbal skills, including comprehension and fluency, tend to develop more slowly at first, increasing more rapidly than other aptitudes as a child gets older. Probably, verbal tests rely on acquired knowledge rather more than many others, and so it is not surprising that this ability be slower to develop.

Sex is another important variable, and men and women do show different aptitudes. Women, for example, tend to be better than men at verbal tasks. At school, girls do better in language subjects; their grammar is more accurate and spelling more consistent. In later life, they are more inclined to learn languages and are frequently to be found in journalism, publishing and similar professions.

In men, visuo-spatial ability is stronger. From an evolutionary point of view this might be explained by the role of men as hunters, who would need a good ability to judge distances, speeds and so on if they were going to bring home the supper. But in our more modern world, boys at school tend to be better than girls at practical subjects and to develop into engineers, mechanics and others who need spatial ability.

There is another interesting relationship between IQ and sex. If we look at the 'normal' distribution of IQ scores for each sex, we find that the distribution for women rises higher in the centre and is less extended at the extremes. There are fewer women at the very top of the IQ scale, but there are fewer women at the very bottom – just as there are not many women company directors or Nobel scientists, while there are not many women on Skid Row.

The phenomenon can once again be explained in evolutionary terms. A population advances and develops when there are variations within it which can be selected naturally. There will be some variations which help survival, others which do not; and from this point of view, the male is more expendable than the female, since one male can father many more offspring than a female can bear. And indeed, we find that most human characteristics, not just IQ, are correlated to sex in the same manner.

There is even a genetic explanation for the phenomenon. The sex of an individual depends upon his or her chromosome nature – males have an X and a Y chromosome, while females have two X chromosomes. Since chromosomes operate in pairs for the most part, the characteristics of each X chromosome in females will be 'diluted' by the genetic material from the other. But in males, the X and Y chromosomes do not operate together, and so the X chromosome has more of an effect on the nature of the individual, not being diluted or moderated by others. Studies of genetics would predict different correlations of IQ and other abilities within families depending on how many chromosomes the relatives have in common — and indeed, the test evidence bears this out.

Intelligence, inheritance and environment

Few subjects have caused such heated debate in the last few years as the question of the degree to which intelligence is inherited from one's parents. So strong have been the opinions on each side that two distinguished proponents of a largely hereditarian theory, Professor H. J. Eysenck of Britain and Professor William Schockley of the United States, have actually found themselves the victims of punches and kicks in academic settings.

The stakes are high in the debate. If it can be demonstrated that the differences in average IQ which we find in individuals, groups or races are the product of upbringing, or principally so, then some people feel this is an argument for the transference of resources to less fortunate — low-IQ — people in order to restore the balance. It is also said that a hereditarian view leads to arrogance and complacency among those on the top strata and in the higher-scoring groups or races, and is in itself a 'racist' fallacy.

In fact there is a strong body of evidence for supposing that intelligence is about 80% due to inheritance; the remaining 20% variation can be put down to environmental conditions. But the issue is very complex. Just as the development of a plant is due not only to the genetic material contained in the seed, but to the environmental conditions through which it is nurtured — heat, light, water and soil composition, for example — so it is difficult to isolate the effects of environment from inheritance in human intelligence. Testing gives us great difficulty; a family are closely related, and so provide a good group in which we can see certain effects of inheritance. But they are also subject to a very similar environment — in the same socio-economic class, with similar interests and friends — so we cannot really isolate the effects very clearly.

Most of the evidence which we do have for saying that intelligence is 80% inherited comes from the study of family groups which have been split up, particularly from the study of identical twins who have been separated from birth. For identical twins have identical genetic complements, and if they show marked variation in IQ when brought up in different environments, then we know that IQ would be mediated primarily by an individual's surroundings, not by his genetic constitution.

But in fact we find that the IQ of identical twins correlates nearly, no matter how they are brought up. On average, their IQs differ by less than seven points; and remember, the same person tested at two different times can show variation on average about five points. So there is a very strong correlation. The age at which the twins were separated does not seem to affect the similarity of score very much.

The coefficient of correlation is a statistical tool used to compare populations. A correlation of 1 implies a perfect match; that individuals in one population are similar in some respect to those in another. With identical twins, we discover a coefficient of correlation of about 0.85 or so – a very high match. With fraternal or non-identical twins, which share only 50% of the same heritable material as opposed to the identical twins' 100%, the IQ scores show a correlation of only 0.55. Other family relationships show again that the IQ correlations are very close to the proportion of genetic material that is shared.

However, it should be remembered that the number of cases we must rely on to make the judgement about identical twins is necessarily small; comparatively few identical twins have been separated early in childhood, brought up in different environments and studied in this way.

But as well as seeking individuals of similar genetic make-up and testing their IQ, it is possible to reach a similar conclusion by bringing up different children in rather similar environments. In an orphanage, for example, children are treated much the same; they share the same dormitories, they receive the same attention, have access to the same toys and books, and have the same nurses and teachers. Were it the case that IQ is shaped largely by environment, the children in such an environment should score roughly equally. But again, when we compare the IQ distribution of children in orphanages with those in the outside world, we find only slightly less (about 10% less) variation.

Another method of isolating the factors is to look at the IQ of children who have been brought up by foster parents, and compare their scores with the scores of their parents. One finds that a fostered child grows up to have a 0.8 correlation with its natural parents by the age of fourteen. But there is almost no correlation between the IQs of children and their foster parents.

All of this evidence goes to suggest most strongly that IQ is about 80% inherited. The most controversial result of this discovery, however, comes when we ask whether there are any national or racial differences in intelligence.

When we take average IQ scores for different groups, we find that there are indeed major variations between them, although in this context it seems that racial differences are not as important as the differences between smaller, regional divisions of people. The American Negro is, on average, fifteen points lower in IQ than the white American, however, and Mexican Americans are midway between these two groups. In Europe, it is well known that the average IQ in southern England is higher than that in the rest of Britain, and about eight points higher than the average in Ireland.

The differences between Britain and Ireland may be a mixture of racial differences and the obvious fact that intelligent people have tended, over the centuries, to drift out of Ireland and towards southern England. But the scores of the American Negro or Mexican American seem to be predominantly racial. Jews score higher than the average Caucasian; Orientals are similarly more intelligent than the white man, so the differences are not all one sided.

As well as having a different average, the black population in America seems to be closely packed around its mean – the spread of IQ is less in Negro populations than in white. This has another effect which helps generate racial strife; the Negro population peaks at about 85 and tails off rapidly as it approaches 110 or so. But the white population in America peaks at just over 100 and is still pretty numerous around 130. So there is a much higher proportion of the white population in the range 100–130 and over than in the Negro, and the proportion gets higher as one goes up.

Consequently, as IQ is roughly correlated with occupational success, there is a much larger proportion of whites than blacks in top positions in America. To those who do not understand that this is a product of different normal distributions, this naturally causes concern.

It is true that there are many ways in which IQ tests can mislead us. One problem is the 'cultural fairness' of the tests. For example, it is often said that Negroes perform less well on verbal tests because of language differences, and that this depresses their IQ score on any test with a high verbal content. (In fact, however, the evidence seems to suggest that blacks perform better than whites on verbal problems, so the argument is not so strong.) But psychologists now have many years of skill in devising test items which are not biased between different cultures.

Nor can the differences in score be dismissed on the grounds of the different expectations of the different populations, due to their different status. For the Mexican American, whose socioeconomic status is lower than that of the American Negro, outperforms him on most tests.

However, the intelligence test certainly does not give us any ground to treat a particular race or group of people differently. There is wide variation among human beings, and there are plenty of intelligent Negroes, Hispanics and Irishmen who are much more able than most Englishmen or white Americans. Similarly, there are plenty of Chinese and Jews who outshine the overwhelming bulk of Caucasians. When we are faced with a particular individual, we have no grounds for supposing that his intelligence is poor because his skin is black. Race may help predict IQ to a certain degree, but it is by no means a useful tool to select people for education or employment or anything else. There are indeed average racial differences; but the measurement of IQ shows us that these differences are so large *within* each race that differences *between* them are popularly overestimated.

Measuring IQ biologically

One of the most exciting developments of the last few years is the prospect that we might be able to obtain an accurate assessment of a person's IQ by examining some of his physical characteristics. The nineteenth-century psychologists found no correlation between such things as brain size or simple reaction times, but nowadays, with more sophisticated tests and measurements, there is a real prospect that this kind of biological measurement of intelligence, already in its infancy, may grow to be a very useful procedure. But this sort of measurement is also controversial; because if it can be shown that IQ has a strong relationship to physical structures in the body, then the variability of IQ due to environmental forces must be rather small, and the hereditarian argument must be substantially correct.

Two major methods of measuring IQ biologically have been identified, although psychologists are working on others. The first and most important kind of analysis concerns physical activity in the human brain, long thought to be associated with intelligence.

The 'brain waves' which scientists can detect follow a fairly common pattern when an individual reacts to a sudden stimulus such as a loud noise or a flash of light. The average evoked potential in the brain cells at first jumps rapidly, then tapers off over the course of a second or less. But the jump and tapering are not steady, and are made up of a series of jerky movements. In the pioneering work on this by J. Ertl, it was shown that the speed of these jerky movements was related to intelligence. Individuals who score high on intelligence tests showed faster waves than duller people. The brain waves of very intelligent people are quick to respond to the stimulus and are rapid; the brain waves of the very dull people are smoother and slower.

But measuring this effect is not easy, and Ertl's own findings in the 1960s were criticised for technical insufficiencies. One great problem is separating out the wave motion we want to detect from all the background jerks, troughs and peaks which the measuring instruments normally detect anyway.

Some fresh work on the phenomenon was done by Eysenck and by Elaine Hendrickson in the same laboratory. Once again, it was found that IQ (in this case using chosen sections of a well-used IQ test that is very accurate) was related to the electrical activity in the brain. In fact, these psychologists found that the amplitude, that is to say the height or depth of the waves, as well as the frequency or rapidity of the waves, did correlate with IQ. The corre-

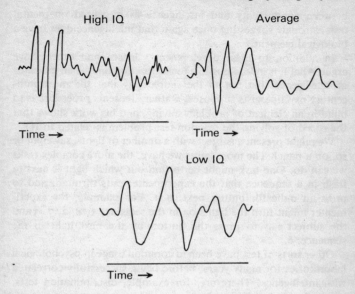

lation is weak at 0.6, but it is definitely positive. The sketch diagram above gives an approximate illustration of the relationship between brainwaves and IQ.

Again it should be stressed that the picture is unclear. Studies by some researchers have found definite correlations between mental agility and brain behaviour, showing that up to 80% of intelligence is physically related or determined. But other researchers have failed to find any correlation whatever. No doubt as experimental procedures improve, the picture will become clearer.

Another way of measuring intelligence physically makes use of the electrical conductivity of a person's skin. Once again, in the 1960s, this measure – the same sort that is used on 'lie detector' tests – was found to be strongly connected with IQ scores. Further work on this is needed. The early research was done on children, and since the skin conductivity of children increases anyway as they grow up, naturally this has to be allowed for. But certainly the work showed a statistically significant correlation between conductivity and intelligence as measured on mental tests, strongly suggesting once again that intelligence does have a biological element.

In addition to these developments, Jensen and others have argued that it is indeed possible to use reaction time as an indicator of intelligence, but not in the simple way that the nineteenth-century psychologists supposed. Rather, Jensen's procedure is to build in an element of problem solving, and his work shows that the speed of solving the reaction-test problem is related to IQ.

We might present a subject with a number of lights, say eight or so, on a panel. The more lights we have, the more complex tasks we can do. One task might be to find out which light is next to flash in a sequence that the experimenter puts through, and to press an indicator button next to it. For example, the experimenter might turn the lights on in the sequence 1, 8, 2, 7, 3 and the subject has to press the button by the next light in the sequence: 6.

Other sorts of test have been in common usage in psychological laboratories for many years, before being successfully correlated with intelligence. There are, for example, discrimination tests, where the subject is shown two figures on a screen or on cards, and asked to push different buttons if they are similar, or different. Some complex decisions can be put forward to the subject — is a large drawing of a fox similar to a small one? Is the figure 4 similar to the roman IV? It is not so much the correctness of any particular answer that is at stake, but how long the subject takes to make up his mind. And once again, subjects who can decide these things quickly tend to have a statistically higher IQ than those who do not. And surprisingly perhaps to the layman, not only do high-IQ people tend to be quicker in making a decision, but they tend to be quicker in making the movements needed to press the button! This again confirms what scientists have long known but what laymen think is completely the opposite — that people with high intelligence also tend to be good at other things including those requiring physical dexterity.

These methods of measuring IQ are, however, new at the moment, and we can only wait and see the new procedures which will undoubtedly arise and the new statistical analyses which they will be subjected to. It should be an exciting time.

Genius and subnormality

The fact that we must exercise a great deal of caution when dealing with intelligence test scores is illustrated by the difficulty of explaining the creativity of a genius, such as a great artist or a great composer, in terms of present theories of intelligence. The IQ score is no more than that; a single figure which summarises a person's mental ability. But it is possible that two people with the same IQ scores can be utterly different in many other ways – in height, in weight, in sex, in shyness and other personality traits. Similarly, people with the same IQ scores can be very different in terms of their ability to create new things, write music, paint pictures, compose poems. Something much more is needed to explain the qualities we call 'genius'.

Personality factors may again provide most of the explanation, just as they explain the different performance of equally intelligent children in school. To be at the height of a creative profession requires drive and commitment to the form being worked upon and created; the artist has to be passionately involved in his field if his contribution is to be noticed and admired. Furthermore, he has to be so committed that he puts other things, even other people, aside. A certain ruthlessness may well be a necessary part of the artistic temperament, and it is well known that great artists, writers or composers have the reputation of being self-centred, vain and uncaring about those who have little interest in their creations.

This may help to explain the sexual differences in the creative arts. If we supposed that the ability to write great music, be a great mathematician or author, were due to extremely high intelligence alone, men would still be at an advantage because, as we have seen, the spread of IQ scores is greater among men and there are very few women at the extremely high (or extremely low) edges. But when we compound this with the personality factors of drive and aggressiveness, typically male characteristics, the men must have a clear edge in the struggle to become the creators and inventors. This male aggressiveness may develop in upbringing rather than through inheritance, some people have argued – but even with considerable opportunity and encouragement, there are surprisingly few instances in which women have reached the great heights of men in professions which are open to all.

Naturally, men are not so graceful as women as ballet dancers; but in fields where mental dexterity is the deciding factor, with one exception, women are rarely numbered among the geniuses. The exception is creative writing, where many great novelists have been women. As we have seen, women do show a greater ability in tests of a verbal nature, and so the number of famous female writers is not surprising: Virginia Woolf, Jane Austen, Mary Shelley, Emily and Charlotte Brontë, George Eliot and so on. But it would be difficult to name a great female scientist outside Madame Curie to put alongside Archimedes, Copernicus, Galileo, Newton, Kepler, Boyle, Watt, Dalton, Rutherford, Darwin and Einstein. The complement of composers – Bach, Beethoven, Brahms, Mozart, Purcell, Rachmaninov, Tchaikovsky, Mendelssohn and so on – is quite without a female representative. The same is true of architects and philosophers, economists and mathematicians. All of this suggests very strongly – *if* we reject the common argument that women lack the opportunity for advancements in these fields and that their valuation of achievement is suppressed in the attitudes of society – that the elements of genius are only partly intelligence, and are quite largely the effect of biological and personality differences between the sexes.

These factors make it very unwise to pick any particular IQ score and declare everyone above it to be a genius, for it is quite possible that people with very high IQs are unmotivated and have no desire to stand out from the crowd. Nor is it possible to deduce a person's IQ from the creative quality of his work; suggestions that Goethe must have had an IQ of 200 and Beethoven of 160 are rather facile. The true factors which underlie such ability are very complex.

Indeed, we still lack any way of assessing these factors, and no satisfactory test of creativity has yet been devised, despite numerous attempts over the last century. There are two main paradigms; one is to give subjects an open-ended question, such as ask them how many ways they can think of to get across a river. Alternatively, we can set problems which require a certain amount of what is commonly called 'lateral thinking', that is, where the answer is not straightforward and requires some thinking around the problem. The difficulty is that neither of these tests is able to distinguish from the rest those people who have shown in outside life that they are able to produce creative work, and indeed the scores on such tests seem to correlate highly with scores on conventional IQ tests. But in any event, it must be remembered that when we are considering the group of people who may be called geniuses, we are dealing with a very small group indeed, and it is difficult to formulate any objective test based on so small a sample. As an IQ score rises, its accuracy diminishes.

The same is true at the lower end of the scale, although there are in fact slightly larger populations at this end of the IQ spectrum. This is because in addition to those who would appear naturally at the lower orders of IQ, there are people who have suffered physical damage (usually to the brain) which depresses IQ, and those who suffer from inborn disorders. Occasionally one finds people who are born into perfectly normal or even intelligent families, but whose IQ is depressed because of a genetic disorder that may 'run in the family' but is seen in relatively few generations because it is recessive. An intellectual impairment may also have a physical component, as in the syndrome known as 'mongolism'. It would be wrong to suppose such individuals to fit naturally on the IQ distribution − there are no physical abnormalities associated with genius, for example − and indeed, they do cause an imbalance. Instead of being the classical, gaussian bell-shaped curve, the IQ distribution in the population has a slight rise on its lower slope.

But once again, the IQ score in itself disguises this issue, and treats everyone below a certain figure, say below 60 or 70, identically. But the impairment might be just the outcome of chance, or might be part of a larger, sometimes physical, disorder. Moreover, there is the case of autistic children and certain other syndromes to consider. On IQ tests, they score very badly, but they can be very able at certain things; for example, music or painting. Autistic children tend to be born into very intelligent families, and one would not predict such a massive fall in IQ in a single generation, even under the principle of regression towards the mean. This has led some people to speculate that such children really are quite intelligent, perhaps highly intelligent, but lack the motivation to display that ability except in certain ways, if at all. So once again, the message is that the statistics mask a great many interesting individual differences under the bell-shaped curve.

The uses of intelligence tests

No comment about intelligence would seem complete if it did not contain the old saw that 'intelligence is what intelligence tests measure'. The maxim does remind us that intelligence is an elusive concept, a global mixture of mental abilities, and that there is more to life than just the ability to do a certain kind of test. Nevertheless, while the test defines only the person's ability to excel in solving certain kinds of problem, it does give us a general, but not entirely reliable, guide to how he or she will perform in outside life. For this reason, intelligence tests have been found to be of value in streaming schoolchildren, prompting people to enter the right kind of profession for them, and selecting those who need mental abilities to occupy special positions within their professions.

Their widespread use makes intelligence tests familiar to a large part of the population, although their importance is not properly appreciated. In schools, tests are used routinely throughout the world to stream children, and this can be done efficiently when the path of the child's intelligence curve over life can be predicted with some accuracy. This is normally around the age of ten or eleven, where factors of physical maturity, home upbringing and the general anxiety of the school environment have settled down, and where the child has acquired a measure of straightforward knowledge of words and numbers which allow him to be tested on problems which make use of these building-blocks. In Britain for a long time, children were tested with the 'eleven-plus' examination, a mixture of an IQ test and a general knowledge test, which had a reasonable rating of accuracy, but which nevertheless needed some revisions at a later age, when children were moved up or down between schools. But the difficulties of basing a judgement about a child's life on just one test posed as many political difficulties as it posed scientific questions.

One of the chief questions raised in objection to such tests is that of learning: a person can usually improve his performance on a test after the first attempt, and performance also improves on the second and even the third test. So if people are exposed to intelligence tests, it seems likely that they will achieve higher IQ scores than those who are not.

Part of the reason for this improvement is anxiety. As

Spearman's definition of intelligence showed, the ability to pull new relationships and new content out of problems was all important. For this reason, IQ tests attempt to ask the subject about things he might not have come across before – alphabetical or numerical patterns and sequences, strange diagrams and so on. They are not composed of knowledge questions such as 'Who won the battle of Hastings?' or 'Who wrote *La Bohème*?' But when faced with a new situation for the first time, almost everyone feels a twinge of anxiety, and some feel it quite intensely; and the intelligence test ought to be a new situation when first presented, because it seeks the production of novel relations in the mind.

If it is possible to improve one's score on an IQ test just by becoming familiar with the kind of question that is asked, the interesting new sequences and diagrams that are presented – and even, in the case of those with very frequent exposure to tests, the way in which testers' minds work and the limits of the complexity contained in most questions – then obviously the use of IQ tests to select children or adults according to mental ability is difficult. Some people will be facing a test for the first time, while others may have had considerable practice on them, and may even enjoy solving the kind of problem that they contain.

How to make tests fair? One way is to make tests infrequently available, not to publish them or be permitted to present them except in test situations. Some of the more established IQ tests are in fact just like this; they are not generally published, and users are expected to use them with care. An IQ test, in addition, costs a great deal in terms of time and money to draw up, check, standardise and print so that it would make nonsense of the exercise if a few subjects could look up the test in the library and work out all the answers in advance! But this approach causes problems. Even the grandest tests seem to be available from somebody. Often, a person will be tested on exactly or roughly the same test at two different times in his life. So it is difficult to avoid a population where some people are familiar with the test questions and others are not, something which is particularly important when we remember that scores increase more between the first test and the second than they do between second and third, third and fourth and so on.

The alternative seems to be to make tests as generally available as possible, in the hope that if people do them for fun or even if they have come across them in earnest, most of the improvement in individual performance due to training and the reduction of anxiety will have lapsed. Fortunately, there are now many books designed to equip the general reader with a grasp of IQ tests and to give him a rough check on his own score – notably the books by Hans Eysenck, Glenn Wilson and, for children, Victor Serebriakoff.

In doing tests of a different nature, such as the various tests in this book, the results of practice may be unpredictable; here, training in problem-solving is mixed with the testing of different abilities, and it is likely that no smooth pattern of improvement will emerge. But when a reader is faced with a number of similar tests, there is a common pattern of improvements. By and large, a person can improve his IQ score by about five or six points between the first test and the second he faces; by about four points between the second and third; and then the improvement tails off until there is probably no improvement at all after the fifth test.

When an IQ test is used for selection, of course, the effect of such training can be crucial. It is at the borderline that those with practice win through over those who have none. So it is to be hoped that the results of practice will become common to everyone as IQ testing grows in reliability and as IQ tests are used more widely still.

But there must still be caution whenever the results of any test are being considered. There is the noticeable effect of practice. There is the question of the reliability of the scores themselves and the accuracy to which the test is standardised: if the test is short, random errors will arise – for example, a highly intelligent subject may achieve a poor score on a short test because he spends too much time figuring out one problem. We also have to remember that there is much more to human character than intelligence alone: a high IQ does not necessarily make anyone a morally upright individual. Nor does the measurement of a low IQ provide a case for forcing individuals, or groups of individuals, into lower occupations or castes. In fact, the proper understanding of intelligence shows us that IQ is so variable within groups, and human personality so variable outside the measure of intelligence, that it ridicules any such kind of idea.

Further reading

There are a number of books of intelligence tests now available, notably those by H. J. Eysenck, *Know Your Own IQ* and *Check Your Own IQ* (published by Pelican Books). Glenn Wilson has also written *Improve Your IQ* and has collaborated with Diana Grylls to produce *Know Your Child's IQ* (both published by Futura). Victor Serebriakoff, the international chairman of the high-IQ society MENSA, has collaborated with Dr Stephen Langer to write *Check Your Child's IQ* (Sphere Books).

Eysenck is also the author of many scholarly works on the subject of intelligence, which are to be recommended. These include the controversial *Race, Intelligence and Education* (Temple Smith), a debate with Leon Kamin entitled *Intelligence: The Battle for the Mind* (Pan Books) and the comprehensive *The Structure and Measurement of Intelligence* (Springer-Verlag).

Instructions for the tests

There are four tests following, which are designed to examine different aspects of your mental abilities. They are:

Test One – Mixed questions: 80 items.
Test Two – Sequences: 80 items.
Test Three – Patterns: 40 items.
Test Four – Puzzles: 40 items.

Each test takes exactly one hour, so you should pick a time when you will not be interrupted and can concentrate fully on the questions.* Measure the time elapsed as accurately as you can, because even a few moments more or less can make a large difference to your score in certain cases. Equip yourself with a pen or pencil and write your answers in the book.

The answer in almost every case is a single number or letter, or a pair of them. You do not have to draw anything, and you do not need any other special ability – just that of problem-solving.

Note down your answers in the book and mark them against the correct answers given at the end. Add up your score and use the tables to convert this into an approximation of your IQ.

Some hints

Pace yourself through the test, so that each question gets enough time. They can usually be solved with a bit of effort, so try more than one way of doing each. On the other hand, do not get bogged down on one particular question, because you might be approaching it quite wrongly and could be doing several other questions in the same time. It is unlikely that you could do all questions in the test. All questions count equally, so there is no advantage in spending excessive time on the more difficult ones.

*If you have difficulty in finding a complete hour, you can divide the tests in half and take half an hour; but you should calculate your IQ only on the basis of the complete test.

If you think that you have the right answer, note it down, even if you are not completely certain about it. But do not make wild guesses. And when checking your score, if you have an alternative answer which you are *sure* is just as good as the one listed as correct, then count it. It is quite common for people to come up with alternative answers which fit all the requirements of the question − often people find a complicated way of tackling a question which can be worked out quite easily. But the IQ tester is usually after the simplest way of solving each problem.

Remember that these tests are principally for amusement; no serious decisions should be made on the result. Also, because the tests measure different things, your IQ score may vary between one and the next. A simple averaging will give you a fair idea of your global ability, but it is important not to take the results too seriously.

BUTLER–PIRIE
Test One

This test is designed to examine your abilities in a range of questions – verbal, numerical, pictorial and logical. Follow the instructions given as you go along, and mark your answers in the spaces provided.

There are 80 questions in all. Now begin.

Time allotted: one hour.

SECTION I – VERBAL

(A) Odd Man Out

Instructions:
Underline in each row the word which is most different in meaning from the others.

e.g. Chair, stool, desk, <u>carpet</u>, table.

Now continue.

1 Truthful, cowardly, pensive, sly, virtuous.

2 Fox, cougar, leopard, wildcat, tiger.

3 Walked, rode, sailed, travelled, flew.

4 Educate, explain, instruct, teach, train.

5 Object, time, room, person, reason.

(B) Word Completion

Instructions:

For each question find the three letters which make words when preceded by the given letters.

e.g.   BR
       FR
       R   _ _ _   ANSWER: <u>I S K</u>
       OBEL
       WH

Now continue.

6   BR
    GL
    H
    L   _ _ _   7   B
    STR   C
    W   DI
                            ER   _ _ _
                            N
                            R

8   BL
    CR
    L
    SP   _ _ _   9   B
    T   C
    WR   H
                            SH   _ _ _
                            TH
                            W

10   B
     CR
     DR   _ _ _
     FL
     P
     T

(C) Synonyms

Instructions:
Underline in each row the word which is nearest in meaning to the given word.

e.g. Threat means nearly the same as
      (blackmail, fear, anger, worry, <u>menace</u>).

Now continue.

11   Remainder means nearly the same as
     (residue, discarded, relic, trace, left).

12   Different means nearly the same as
     (irregular, abnormal, unlike, strange, unusual).

13   Lithe means nearly the same as
     (agile, able, quick, athletic, supple).

14   Tempt means nearly the same as
     (allure, intrigue, suggest, cajole, entice).

15   Plea means nearly the same as
     (question, request, demand, requisition, petition).

(D) Antonyms

Instructions:
Underline in each row the word which is most nearly opposite in meaning to the given word.

e.g. Hot is the opposite of
      (damp, chilly, <u>cold</u>, bleak, windy).

Now continue.

16   Exclude is the opposite of
     (admit, count, receive, register, allow).

17 Approach is the opposite of
(distant, depart, leave, diminish, recede).

18 Limited is the opposite of
(unbounded, uncontrolled, free, liberal, unregulated).

19 Hurt is the opposite of
(restore, heal, atone, help, benefit).

20 Disagree is the opposite of
(match, settle, concur, consent, accede).

SECTION II – NUMERICAL

(A) Analogies

Instructions:
Fill in the missing number in each question.

e.g.

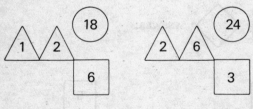

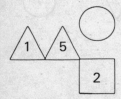

ANSWER: 12

Now continue.

21

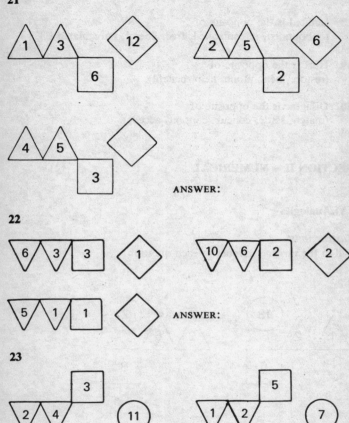

ANSWER:

22

ANSWER:

23

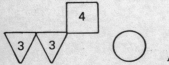

ANSWER:

24

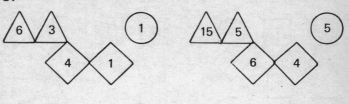

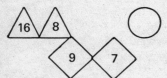

ANSWER:

25

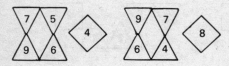

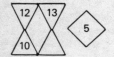

ANSWER:

26

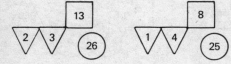

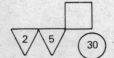

ANSWER:

27

6	2	(8)

(4)

4	3	(1)

(7)

7	5	(4)

ANSWER:

28

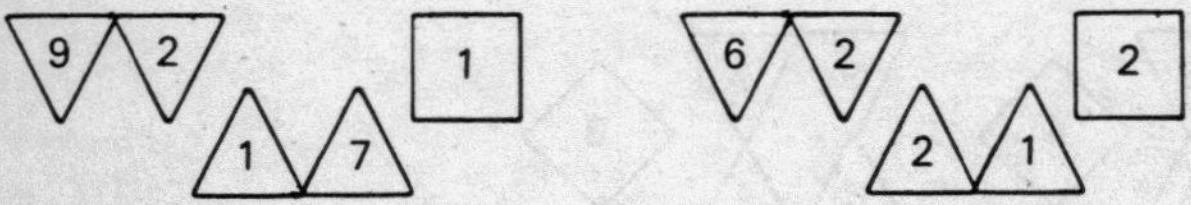

9 2 · 1 7 · 1

6 2 · 2 1 · 2

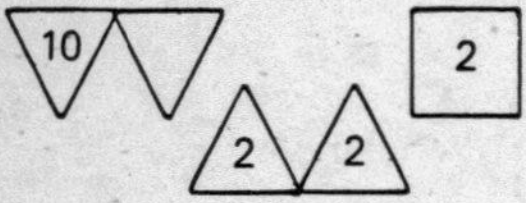

10 · 2 2 · 2

ANSWER:

29

| 3 | | 4 | 1 | 63 |

| 4 | | 5 | 4 | 369 |

| | | 8 | 2 | 60 |

ANSWER:

30

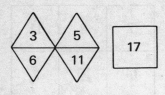 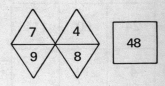

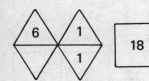

ANSWER:

(B) Grids

Instructions:

Fill in the missing number in each of the figures. The same rule of arithmetic links each bottom number with the one above it.

e.g.

1	3	4
2	4	

The missing number is 5, each number being one greater than the number above it.

Now continue.

31

4	6	8
6	8	

32

55	44	33
5	4	

33

24	60	114
4	10	

34

7	8	11
14	16	

35

4	7	9
11	14	

36

12	6	21
16	8	

37

2	9	3
6	27	

38

16	12	4
28	21	

39

11	4	7
30	9	

40

4	9	8
-54	36	

SECTION III – PICTORIAL

(A) Analogies

Instructions:

For each question, identify the figure which completes the relationship.

e.g.

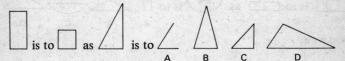

ANSWER: C

41

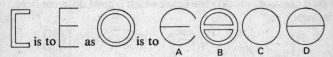

ANSWER:

42

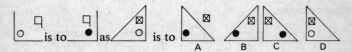

ANSWER:

43

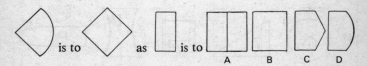

ANSWER:

44

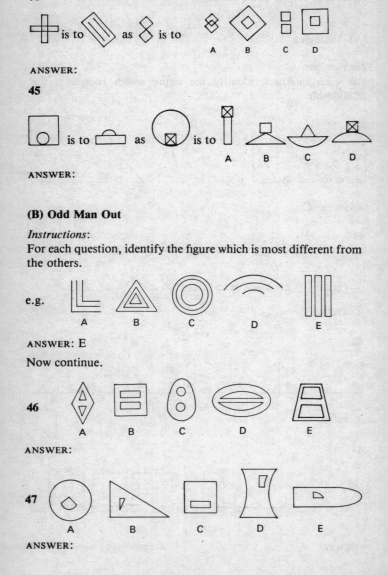

ANSWER:

45

ANSWER:

(B) Odd Man Out

Instructions:

For each question, identify the figure which is most different from the others.

e.g.

ANSWER: E

Now continue.

46

ANSWER:

47

ANSWER:

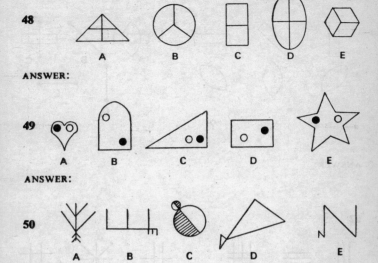

48

A   B   C   D   E

ANSWER:

49

A   B   C   D   E

ANSWER:

50

A   B   C   D   E

ANSWER:

(C) Pattern Completion

Instructions:

For each question pick out the figure which completes the given pattern.

e.g.

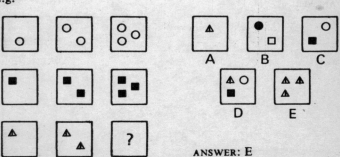

ANSWER: E

51 Now continue.

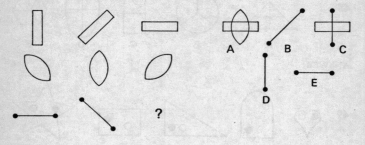

ANSWER:

52

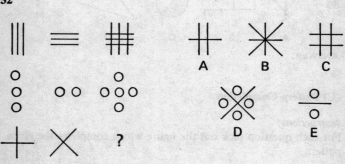

ANSWER:

53

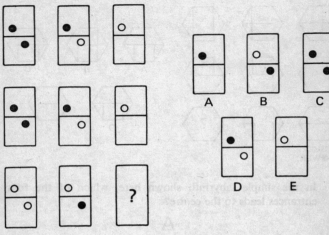

ANSWER:

54

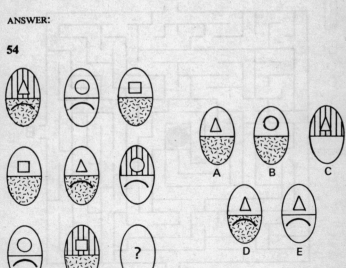

ANSWER:

55

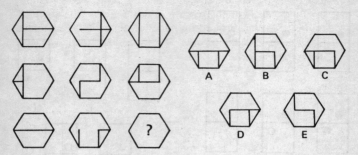

ANSWER:

56 In the simple labyrinth shown here, which of the four entrances leads to the centre?

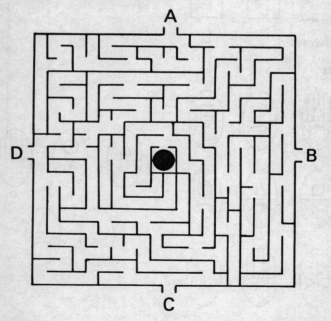

ANSWER:

57 Four tractors make their way home each night at 9 p.m. Tractor A travels at a speed of 20 mph; tractor B at 10 mph; tractor C at 15 mph; tractor D at 12 mph. The tractors' routes take them around the edges of the fields. If each field is a perfect square of side 440 yards long, which tractor arrives home first?

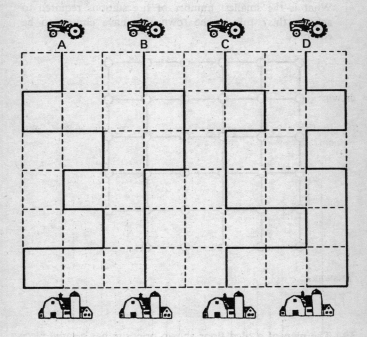

ANSWER:

58 The diagram below represents a simplified map of the 35 towns in a certain country. The circles represent the towns, and the lines represent roads. The distance by road from any town to the next is five miles. The country's leader has promised certain towns with fire stations so that no town is more than five miles by road from its nearest fire station. What is the smallest number of fire stations required to achieve this? Ink in the town you have chosen to be equipped.

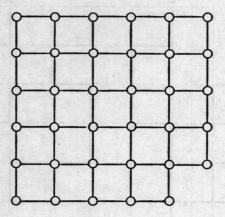

ANSWER:

59 The plan of a tiled floor shown opposite has a large piece missing. Each tile is lettered following a logical sequence. Which group of tiles must be chosen to complete the floor?

ANSWER:

X	B	V	D	T	F	R	H	P	J
A	W	C	U	E	S	G	Q	I	O
N	L	L	N	J	P	H	R	F	T
K	M	M	K	O	I	Q	G	S	E
D	V	B			Z	X	B	V	D
U	C	W				W	C	U	
T	F	R				L	L	N	
E	S	G				M	M	K	
J	P	H	R	F	T	D	V	B	X
O	I	Q	G	S	E	U	C	W	A

a

X	Z		
A	Y	Y	A
P	H	N	J
I	Q	O	K

b

A	Y		
Z	A	Y	A
E	P	J	N
I	Q	K	O

c

X	Z		
A	Y	Y	A
H	P	J	N
Q	I	O	K

d

Z	X		
K	O	Q	I
P	H	N	J
K	O	Q	I

60   The closed tin box which is illustrated below may be constructed from the shaped cutout of thin sheet metal which is shown alongside it, by bending along the dotted lines where necessary. Three of the cutouts which are shown below the figure can similarly be used to construct the same box. Which one(s)?

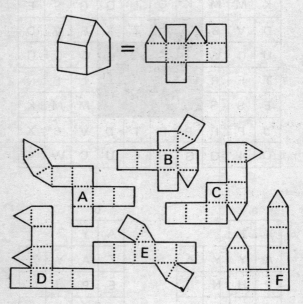

ANSWER:

SECTION IV – LOGICAL RELATIONSHIPS

(A) Word Pairs

Instructions:
Insert the word which means the same as the word outside the brackets.

e.g. SHOOT (. . . .) BLAZE   ANSWER: FIRE

Now continue.

61 IMPOST (. . .) FATIGUE

62 WILLING (. . . .) SPORT

Instructions:
Insert the word which completes the first word and begins the second.

e.g. RING (. . .) TER   ANSWER: LET

Now continue.

63 RO (. . .) ARY

64 MOR (. . .) GET

65 BR (. . .) LING

(B) Word Analogues

Instructions:
Insert the missing word.

e.g. TROT (TRAP) APEX
     CLAP (. . . .) OGLE   ANSWER: CLOG

Now continue.

66 BREAK (RENT) UNTOLD
     CLICK (. . . .) AMENDS

67 SING (GIRL) RULE
     GARB (. . . .) CAKE

68 LAMB (BLED) DOLE
     ARAB (. . . .) EARL

Instructions:
Find the odd man out.

69	HEPES	**70**	BLEAT
	OWC		CREPTA
	ROSEH		HAIRC
	GENNUPI		SKED

(C) Puzzles

71 Of the pupils in the class, 50% have black hair, and 25% have blond hair. 33% are girls, and 67% are boys. Which of the following are definitely true?

(a) The blond-haired pupils are all boys.
(b) Some boys have black hair.
(c) Some blonde-haired pupils are girls.
(d) Both girls and boys have black hair.
(e) Some girls have blonde hair, some have black hair.

ANSWER:

72 A man buying cigarettes which cost £1 handed the tobacconist a £10 note. Having no change, the tobacconist changed it at the next-door grocers, and handed the man £9 change on his return. When the man had gone, the grocer came in, saying the £10 note was a forgery; and the tobacconist had to replace it. How much did the tobacconist lose?

(a) £9   (b) £10   (c) £20   (d) nothing.

ANSWER:

73 The twelve words below may be put into pairs to produce well-known words or phrases. List the words or phrases so formed.

FOOT, BACK, GREEN, LASH, STROKE, HOUSE, LAND, SUN, FINGERS, ICE, BALL, EYE.

ANSWER:

74 A man has nine gold coins. He knows that one of the coins is underweight. By using a beam balance (which weighs one pan against the other), what is the minimum number of weighings he must perform in order to locate the underweight coin?

ANSWER:

75 On a gravestone at Alencourt, near Paris, appears the following inscription:

> Here lies son; here lies mother;
> Here lies daughter; here lies father;
> Here lies sister; here lies brother;
> Here lies wife and husband.

If step-relationships are included, what is the minimum number of persons who must be buried there for the inscription to be accurate?

ANSWER:

76 Two space-rockets approach each other. One travels at 42,000 mph, the other at 18,000 mph. They start 3,526 miles apart; how far are they apart one minute before impact?

ANSWER:

77 Robinson spent one sixth of his money on a book, three times as much on food; and he paid his friend the £5 he owed him. He gambled the rest on a horse, and managed to double his money when it won. When he arrived home he found that he had lost £5, as he had only £1 left. How much did he start with?

ANSWER:

78 One beaker contains water, another wine. If a small quantity of water is transferred to the wine beaker, and the same amount of the resultant mixture is transferred back to the water beaker, is there now more water in the wine than there is wine in the water?

ANSWER:

79 A bank clerk mistakenly switched the pounds and pence when cashing a cheque for a customer. After buying a box of matches for five pence, the customer found he had exactly twice as much as his original cheque. What was the value of the cheque?

ANSWER:

80 A quadrant contains an inscribed rectangle ABCD as shown. Given the distances marked, what is the length of AD?

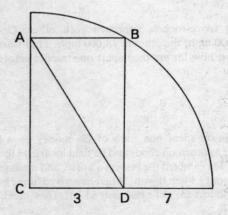

ANSWER:

BUTLER–PIRIE
Test Two

This test is made up from a number of sequences
which test your verbal and numerical abilities.

There are 80 questions in all. Now begin.

Time allotted: one hour.

Instructions:

Each of the following sequences follows a regular rule. Write
down the numbers or letters which will complete the sequences
and replace the question marks. Write your answers clearly alongside each question mark.

e.g. 1   2   4   8   16   ?

ANSWER: 32 (the figure doubles each time).

Now continue.

1   B   D   F   H   ?

2   S   V   Y   B   ?

3   A   Z   C   X   B   ?

4   B   C   H   I   N   ?   ?

5   A   E   J   P   ?

6   T   S   Q   N   ?

7   M   N   J   Q   G   ?

8   U   B   I   P   ?

9   H   V   G   T   F   R   ?   ?

10   J   E   Z   U   ?

11

12

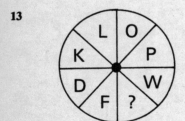

13

14

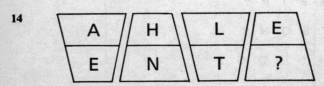

15

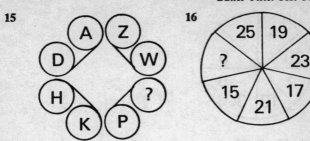

16

17

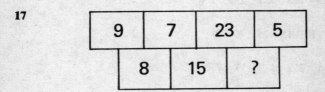

18

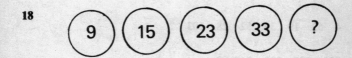

19

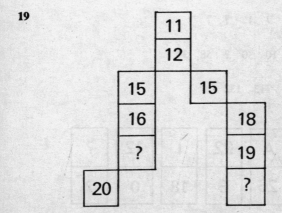

20

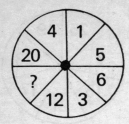

21 7 9 13 ? 37

22 285 253 221 189 ?

23 5 10 15 25 40 ?

24 3⅔ 2⅓ 1 −⅓ ?

25 2 3 5 8 13 ?

26 4 52 19 39 52 28 103 ?

27 905 576 329 247 ?

28 12 8 14 7 16 ? ?

29 9 6 16 10 30 ? 58 34

30 68 81 ? 113 132

31

A	22	I	12	?
26	E	18	0	?

32

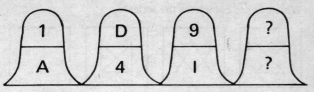

1	D	9	?
A	4	I	?

33

B	J	Q	E	?
2	10	17	?	8

34

```
    ?   Y
  A       U
  E       Q
    I   M
```

35

```
    I  J
  H      K
  Q      T
    ?  S
```

36 Which figure completes the series?

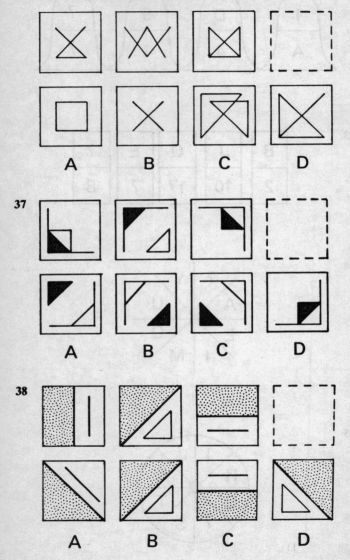

39

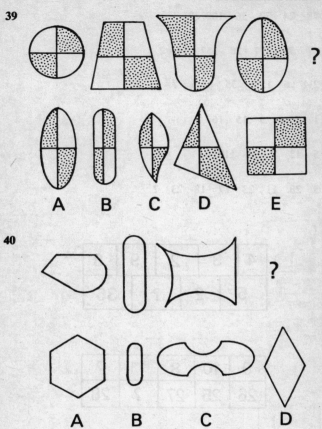

A   B   C   D   E

40

A   B   C   D

41   8723   3872   2387   ?

42   3   12   48   192   ?

43   9   4   8   5   7   6   ?   ?

44   5   7   11   19   35   ?

45   48   24   72   36   108   ?

46   87   56   177   28   357   14   ?

47   2½   6   15½   35   65½   ?

48   1   2   8   9   15   16   ?

49   5   12   ?   54   110

50   5   28   11   23   17   18   23   ?

51

4	3	2	9	8
5	2	?	35	

52

9	10	8	11	?
26	25	27	?	28

53

54

19	25	32
14		?
10		49
7		

55

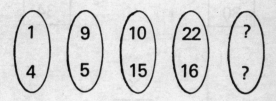

1	9	10	22	?
4	5	15	16	?

56

C	F	I	L	?
X	U	R	O	?

57

58

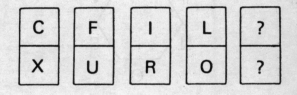

3	1	9	6	12	4
3	11	5	8	0	?

59

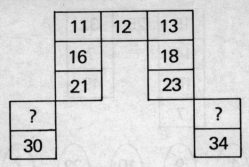

	11	12	13	
	16		18	
	21		23	
?				?
30				34

60

X
?   V
N   S
Q

61 A 7 H 4 L 11 W 1 ?

62 DK MH LO ??

63 A C B E C G D ? ?

64

A	L	?	P	I
J	C	N	G	?

65

L	N	?	U
D	F	I	?

66 2   5   9   14   20   ?

67 53   48   50   45   47   ?

68 1   2   5   26   ?

69 5   8   7   6   10   3   ?

70 0   16   64   144   ?

71 3   8   ?   21

72 0   3   15   63   ?

73 381   378   373   366   ?

74 11   17   29   53   ?

75 2   9   28   ?

76   Which figure below completes the series?

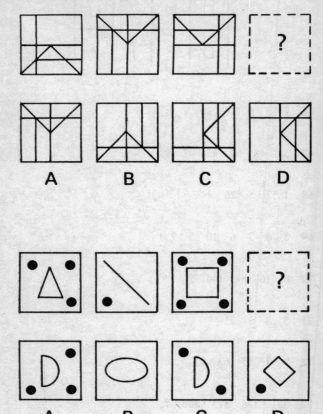

78

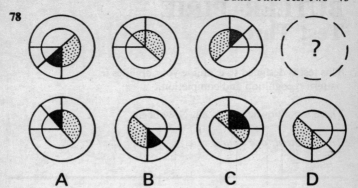

79

3	8	2	9
14	9	6	17
19	1	4	?

80

10	18	34	66	?

BUTLER–PIRIE
Test Three

This test is designed to examine your abilities in pattern recognition and completion.

There are 40 questions in all. Now begin.

Time allotted: one hour.

Instructions:
Each of the following groups of figures follows a regular sequence or pattern, but is incomplete. Which of the figures in brackets will complete the sequence – A, B, C, D, E or F?

e.g.

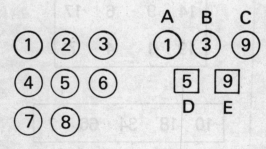

ANSWER: C (The numbers in each row increase by one – or if you prefer, the numbers in each column increase by three. All are in circles.)

Mark your answers clearly alongside the question mark (?) in each pattern.

Now continue.

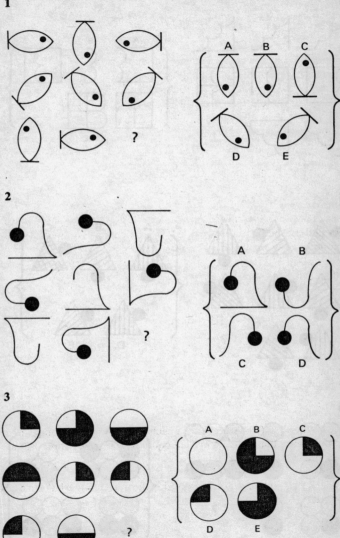

4

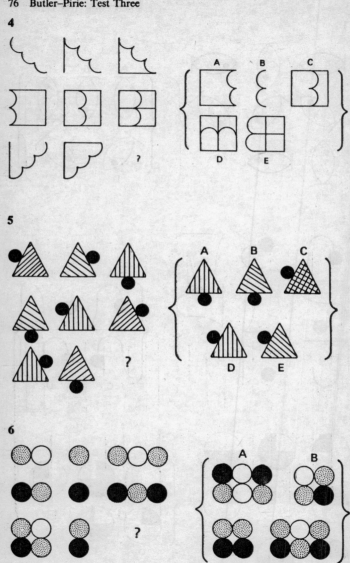

5

6

7

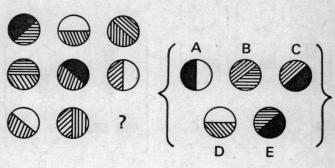

8

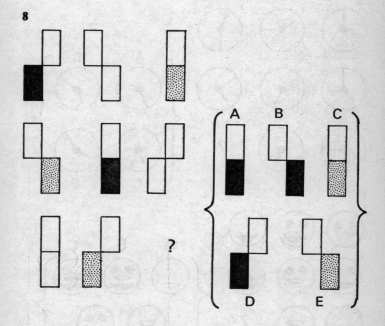

9

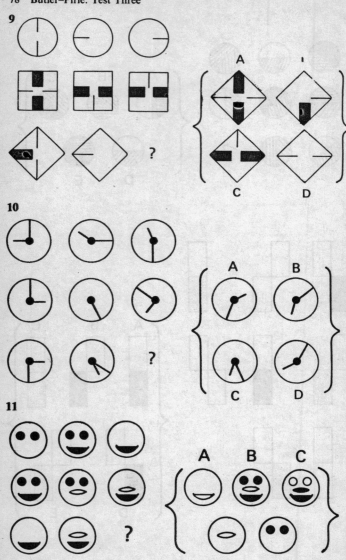

10

11

12

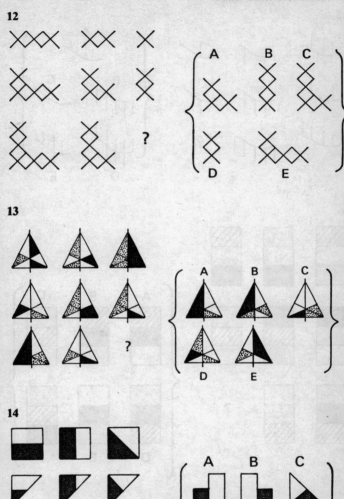

13

14

15

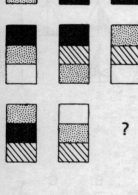

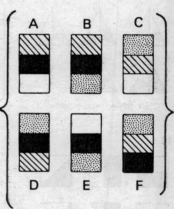

16

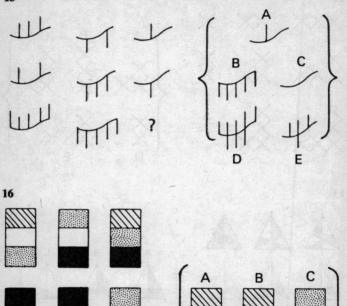

17

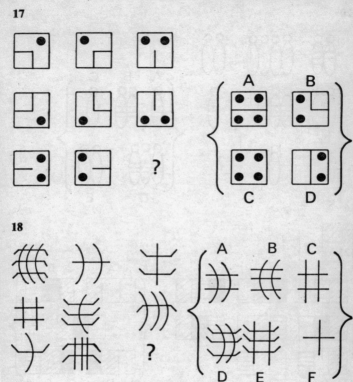

18

19

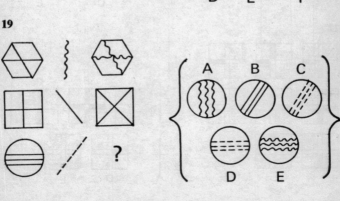

20

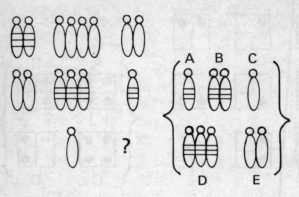

21

22

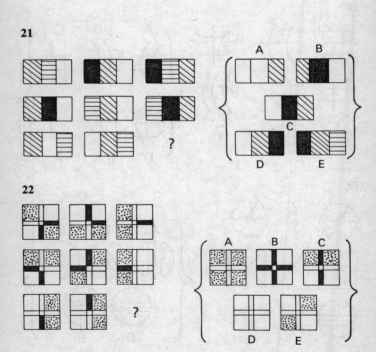

23

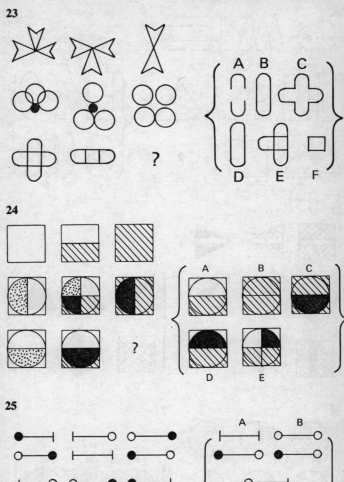

24

25

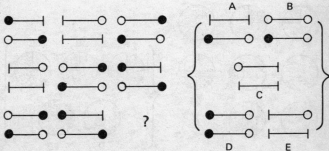

26

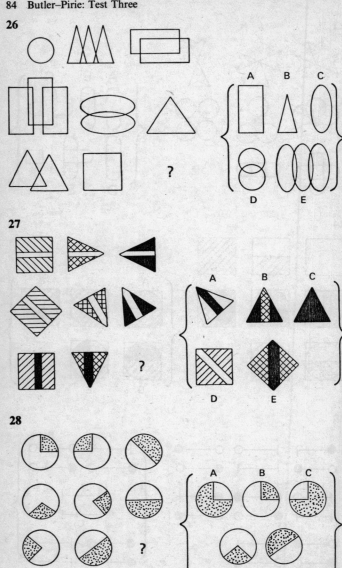

27

28

29

30

31

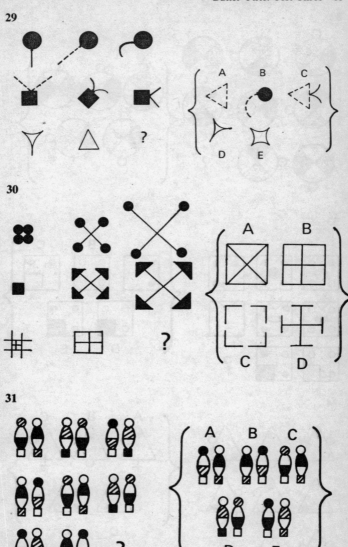

32

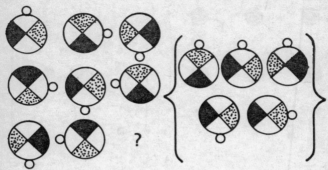

33

34

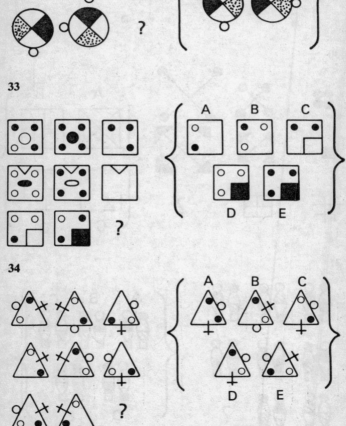

35

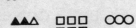

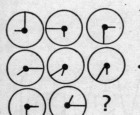

36

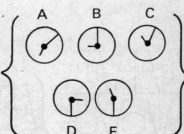

37

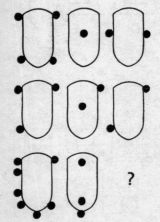

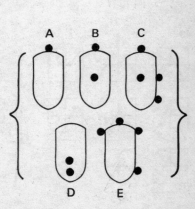

38

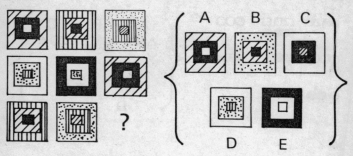

39

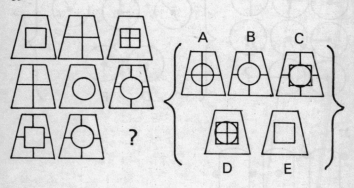

40

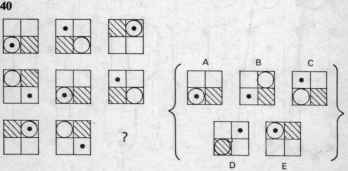

BUTLER–PIRIE
Test Four

This test examines your ability to solve puzzle questions.

There are 40 questions in all. Now begin.

Time allotted: one hour.

Instructions:
Follow the instructions given on each question, and mark your answer in the spaces provided.

1 In the labyrinth shown on the right, which of the six entrances leads to the star?

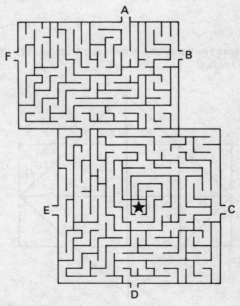

ANSWER:

2 Two of the five drawings to the left are different views of the same die. Given that opposite sides must always add up to seven, which two are these?

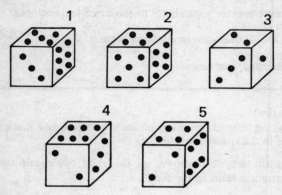

1   2   3

4   5

ANSWER:

3 How many squares and how many triangles are there in the figure below?

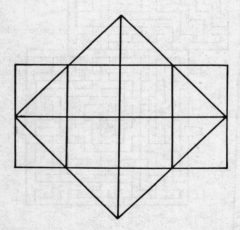

ANSWER:

4 The mechanism illustrated below consists of 14 identical rubber wheels, each fixed on its own axle. Each wheel is free to rotate, but where it touches an adjoining wheel, friction demands that the two wheels turn together in the manner of cog-wheels.

It can be seen that the mechanism is seized up at present. Some wheels have to be removed so that all those remaining can turn smoothly. Show how to do this, leaving the greatest possible number of wheels. Mark the wheels to be removed with an X.

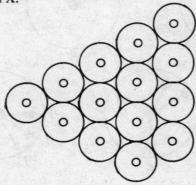

5 The diagram below contains a short sentence which can be read by finding the 'start' letter, and moving one space at a time, horizontally or vertically, but not diagonally. No letter is used more than once. What does the sentence say?

H	A	E	A	H	O
O	R	S	E	S	R
E	S	R	M	I	N
A	H	O	Y	K	G
R	O	F	M	O	D

ANSWER:

6 On the peculiar clock shown here, the hands move in an unusual way. Discover the system as revealed by the four clock positions shown, and draw accurately the fifth in the series.

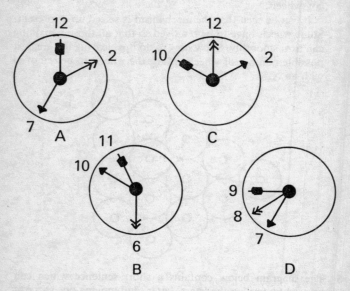

ANSWER:

7   The scale of the figure below is 1 inch = 1 mile.

   The four honey bees shown have lost their way and are trying to return to their hives. By chance they have all picked up the same quantity of pollen, but lose ten grains every five minutes. All travel at a speed of 6 mph. Which bee retains most pollen at the end of its journey?

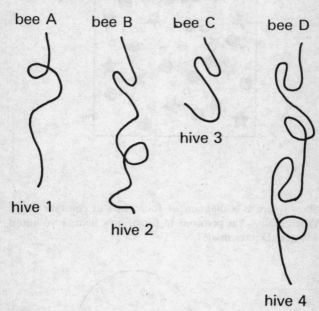

bee A   bee B   bee C   bee D

hive 1   hive 2   hive 3   hive 4

ANSWER:

8   The four drawings below are of the same toy alphabet cube, which has a letter on each of its six faces. Complete the fourth view, D, by correctly drawing in the missing letter.

A   B   C   D

9 Divide the picture below by drawing only straight lines so that there are three circles, three stars and three squares in each section.

10 Shown here is a diagram of four gears in constant mesh. When gear A has revolved 15 times, how many revolutions will gear D have made?

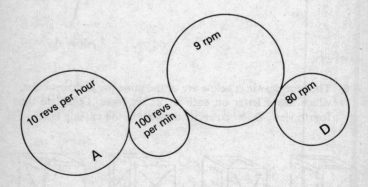

ANSWER:

11 In the maze shown, what is the least number of lines which must be crossed in getting from A to B?

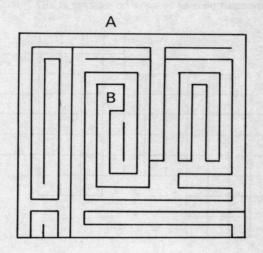

ANSWER:

12 In this coded message from Mensa, the high-IQ society, each letter is represented by either of two symbols. Solve the code and read the sentence.

ANSWER:

13 This is a ground plan for a kitchen which we wish to cover with lino. The lino, however, is cut in definite shapes. Which shape must be used to leave no wastage at all?

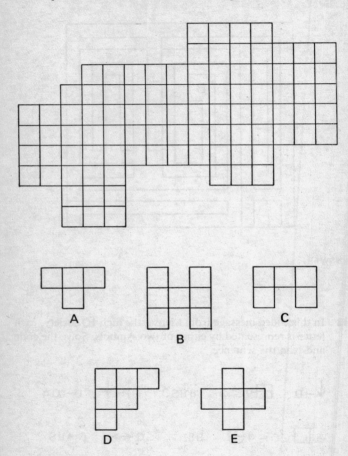

A

B

C

D

E

ANSWER:

14   On this unusual dartboard, what is the least number of darts which could be used to score exactly 100?

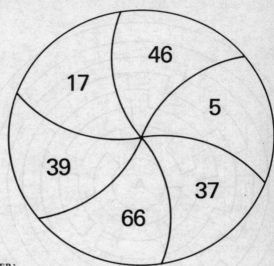

ANSWER:

15   The ancient game of Periwinkle is played just like Noughts & Crosses, except that in Periwinkle the first player to get three in a row (horizontally, vertically or diagonally) loses instead of winning. The figures illustrate two different games of Periwinkle, in each of which it is your turn to go. Mark in your best possible move in each game.

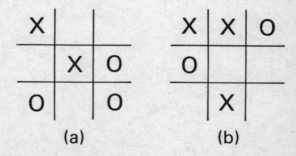

16   In this circular maze, what is the least number of lines which
have to be crossed to get from A to B?

ANSWER:

17 By following the same rules which established the distances shown, how many miles is it to Peking?

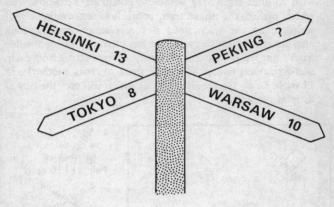

ANSWER:

18 Two of the cardboard shapes shown will fit together to make a perfect square without leaving any gaps. Which two?

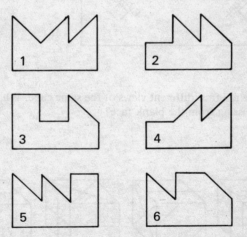

ANSWER:

19 A boy is building a model railway layout. He has built four single-track stations in the positions shown, and does not wish to alter them. He wishes to construct a track layout which provides a direct train route between every pair of stations, so the train need not reverse or pass through another station on the way. He has plenty of plain, flexible track, but no points or crossovers. Points cost £1.50 each, and crossovers (which allow one track to cross another) cost £1 each. Draw the required layout which will cost the boy as little as possible.

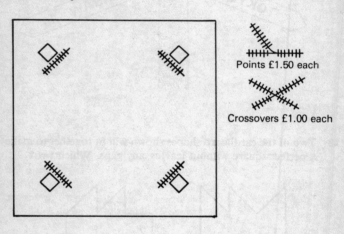

Points £1.50 each

Crossovers £1.00 each

20 Here are four different views of the same cube. What design is missing from the blank face?

ANSWER:

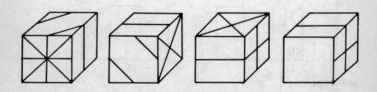

21 This sheet of patterned lino is to be cut into a number of pieces without any wastage. The pieces obtained must all be identical, and the lino must only be cut along the lines of the pattern. Subject to these simple rules, which three of the pieces shown below the large sheet could be produced from it?

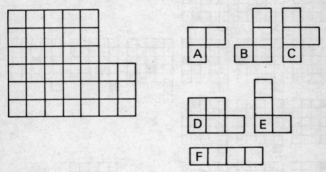

ANSWER:

22 The outermost planet revolves round the sun in 27 weeks; the next one in 9 weeks; and the innermost planet in 1 week. All three orbits are in the same plane, all planets revolve in the same direction, and the sun is at the centre of each orbit. What is the least number of weeks which must elapse before the sun and the planets are in a straight line again?

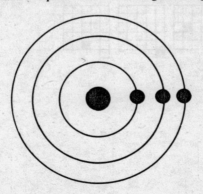

ANSWER:

23 The message below is written in code. Break the code and read the message.

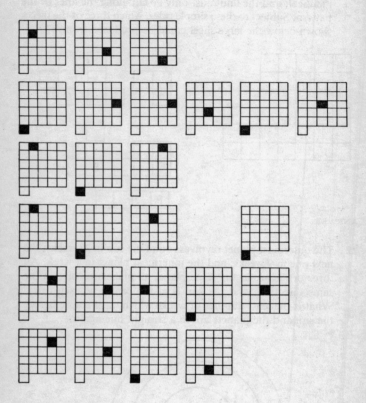

ANSWER:

24 The diagram shown is the simplified plan of a railway system, showing lines and points. How many different routes are there for a train to go from station A to station B without reversing?

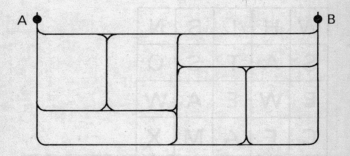

ANSWER:

25 A wall is to be covered with 36 square tiles arranged as shown. Only black and white tiles are available, and there must be no straight rows (horizontal, vertical or diagonal) of three adjacent white tiles. Subject to this rule, what is the smallest number of black tiles required?

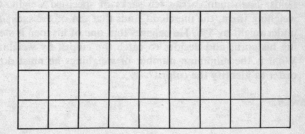

ANSWER:

26   Amongst these letters there is a coiled sentence. However, three letters are not used. What is the hidden sentence?

ANSWER:

W	H	I	S	N			
S	A	T	S	O			
E	W	E	A	W			
C	E	A	M	X			
L	E	R	Y	H	A	L	I
F	S	B	M	A	D	B	T
E	T	I	A	L	E	L	T

27   A merchant employs ten men to fetch his corn from the fields. Each man carries ten sacks of specified weight. On weighing them, the merchant finds that ten of the sacks are underweight by 5%. He believes that one of his men is stealing his corn, and decides to catch the culprit by weighing. What is the minimum number of weighings he must do in order to identify the culprit?

ANSWER:

28 The prison governor, being a member of Mensa, decides to release the cleverest of his three prisoners. He shows them three black discs and two white ones, and tells them that each prisoner will have a disc pinned to his back, with the other two being pocketed. In fact he pins a black one on each prisoner, and pockets the two white ones, without allowing anyone to see which discs were unused. Each prisoner can now see the black discs on his companions' backs, but not his own. The governor announces that he will release the first prisoner who can identify the colour of the disc on his back, and give his reasons. After a quarter of an hour one prisoner steps forward and gives the correct answer. What reason does he give?

ANSWER:

29 A mathematician, when walking very slowly down a descending escalator, reached the bottom after taking 50 steps. Then running up the escalator, one step at a time, he took 125 steps. If the mathematician ran up five times faster than he walked down, how many steps would be visible if the escalator were turned off?

ANSWER:

30 In a room measuring 30 feet × 12 feet × 12 feet (a cuboid), there is a spider in the middle of one of the smaller walls, one foot from the top. On the opposite wall rests a fly, also in the middle, but one foot from the bottom. What is the shortest distance which the spider must crawl in order to reach the fly?

ANSWER:

31   Smith, Jones and Browne are part-time students at a college. They each study two of the following subjects: English Literature, Physics, Car-mechanics, Chemistry, Maths and French. The following also is known:

- The Physics student lives near the Chemistry student.

- The Chemistry student meets both Smith and the one studying Maths in the canteen after classes.

- Browne is younger than Jones but older than the English Literature student.

- The Physics student owes £5 to the Maths student.

- Jones wishes he had studied Maths instead of French.

- The English Literature student asked the one doing Car-mechanics to service his car.

Which subjects are each of them studying?

ANSWER:

32   Peter bought four bottles of beer and Fred bought one of lager. The lager cost twice as much per bottle as the beer. Jack bought nothing, but paid 50p for his share of the drink which they mixed together in a jug and shared out equally. If Jack's 50p covered the full cost of his share, what was the cost of the lager?

(a) 50p   (b) 75p   (c) 30p   (d) 46p   (e) 55p

ANSWER:

33   All tyres are rubber. All rubber is flexible. Some rubber is black. Which two of the following five statements are true?

(a) All tyres are flexible and black.

(b) All tyres are black.

(c) Only some tyres are rubber.

(d) All tyres are flexible.

(e) All tyres are flexible and rubber.

ANSWER:

34 A farmer plants four equal-sized fields with seed, but forgets which field has been planted with which type of seed. He knows, however, that the north field is growing turnips. The other fields contain either wheat or barley. Which two of the following can he say with certainty?

(a) The east field is growing barley.

(b) The south and west fields are both growing barley and wheat.

(c) At least two thirds of his crop will be barley and wheat.

(d) At least one third of his crop is turnips.

(e) No field grows both wheat and barley.

ANSWER:

35 The ten-pence coin is silver; the two-pence coin is brown; the £1 coin is gold. Assuming you paid two coins for an article, and then discovered that if you had bought six you could have paid for those with two coins: which one of the following combinations of coins would be used for the two purchases?

(a) 1. silver and brown   2. two silver

(b) 1. two silver   2. one silver and one gold

(c) 1. two brown   2. two silver

(d) 1. silver and brown   2. two silver

(e) 1. two silver   2. one brown and one gold

ANSWER:

36   My clock has been overhauled by an incompetent amateur. Although the hour hand now works perfectly, the minute hand runs anti-clockwise at constant speed, crossing the hour hand every 80 minutes. If my clock shows the correct time at 6.30, when does it next show the right time?

ANSWER:

37   If a balloon flies at a speed of 28 mph, an airship at a speed of 16 mph, a dove at 20 mph, a goose at 35 mph, and an eagle at 25 mph, at what speed does a hornet fly?

ANSWER:

38   I bought some plates at a recent jumble sale. When I examined them closely at home, I found that two thirds of them were chipped, half were cracked, and a quarter were both chipped and cracked. Only two were without chips or cracks. How many plates did I buy altogether?

ANSWER:

39   Mary and Jane shopped together for sweets with 66p between them. Mary started out with 6p more than Jane, but spent twice as much as Jane. Mary finished up with two thirds as much money as Jane. How much did Jane spend?

ANSWER:

40   When a balloon is filled with argon it can lift one pound of lead at a rate of 55 inches per minute. It can lift the same weight at a rate of 48 inches per minute when filled with neon. When filled with helium it can lift the weight at 68 inches per minute; and with xenon at 72 inches per minute. At what rate of inches per minute can the balloon lift one pound of lead when it is filled with hydrogen?

ANSWER:

Converting your score to IQ

When you have worked out your score on each test, you can convert it into a rough IQ score by using the following tables. For each test, trace horizontally from your score to the line, and then trace vertically downward to arrive at your IQ.

Important

IQ scores are subject to wide variations and can really be assessed only by using sophisticated tests under controlled conditions, sometimes over a period of time. These IQ charts should therefore really be fuzzy lines rather than hard ones, and the results should be considered as only for fun rather than a definite score of IQ. Under no circumstances should personal decisions be made on the basis of scores achieved in these tests.

Test One

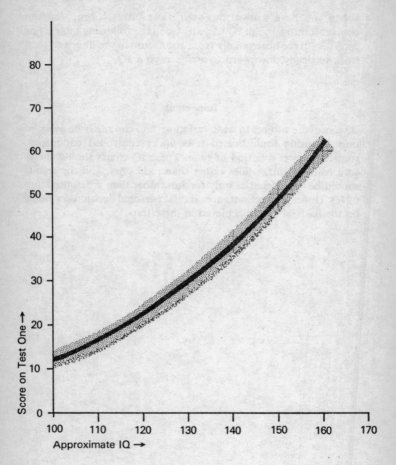

Test Two

Test Three

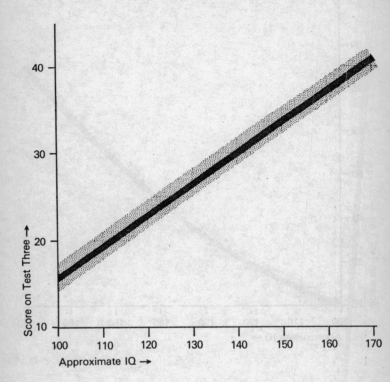

Test Four

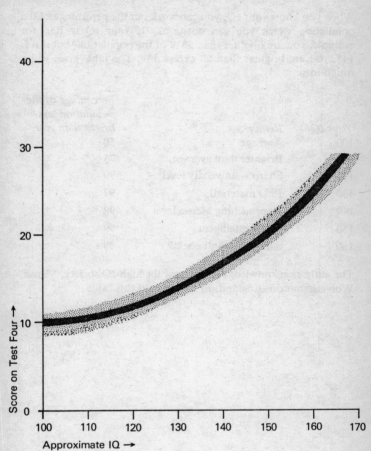

What your IQ means

When you know your IQ, you can work out the percentage of the population which you can out-think. If your IQ is 100, for example, you are brighter than 50% of the population, but if it is 145, you are brighter than all except 1%. The table gives you a rough idea:

Your IQ	Remarks	Percentage of the population less bright than you
100	Average	50
110	Brighter than average	75
120	Sharp – university level	90
130	PhD material!	97
140	Approaching Mensa level	98
150	Super-intelligent	99
160	Sure you didn't cheat?	99 +

The authors acknowledge the help of the high-IQ society, Mensa, Wolverhampton, England, in drawing up this table.

Answers: Test One

1   Pensive (a mood: the others are character traits).

2   Fox (the others are cats).

3   Travelled (the others are specific ways of travelling).

4   Explain (only this does not necessarily imply the presence of a student).

5   Room (all are answers to the questions 'who? what? when? where? why?' but only *room* is non-generic).

6   AND

7   ODE

8   EAK

9   ORN

10 IER

11 Residue

12 Unlike

13 Supple (not *agile*, as is often supposed).

14 Entice

15 Request

16 Admit

17 Recede (*depart* and *leave* imply movement from a starting-place, which *recede* does not).

18 Unbounded

19 Heal

20 Concur

21 3 (multiply each number in the triangles by the number in the square and find the difference).

22 4 (find the difference between the numbers in triangles and divide by the number in the square).

23 13 (multiply the figures in triangles, add the one in the square).

24 4 (divide the difference between the triangles by the difference between the diamonds to get the number in the circle).

25 5 (the sum of the top figures divided by the difference between the bottom figures gives the figure in the diamond).

26 1 (add the squares of the numbers in triangles to the number in the box to reach the number in the circle).

27 6 (the difference in the squares of the boxed numbers equals the product of those in the circle and the diamond).

28 2 (the difference between the numbers in the top triangles divided by the product of the others is the number in the box).

29 2 (the figure in the triangle is the difference in the numbers in circles when raised to the power in the square. Thus $4^3 - 1^3 = 63$; $5^4 - 4^4 = 369$; and $8^2 - 2^2 = 60$).

30 18 (add the squares of the top figures and then subtract the sum of the bottom figures to reach the answer in the box).

31 10 (the numbers increase by 2 with each step rightwards).

32 3 (the top row increases in steps of 11, the bottom in steps of 1).

33 19 (the top row is six times the bottom row).

34 22 (the bottom row is twice the top row).

35 16 (add 7 to the top row to get the bottom).

36 28 (add a third to the figures on the top row to get the figures on the bottom).

37 9 (the bottom row is three times larger than the top).

38 7 (each bottom row number is 1¾ the size of the one above).

39 18 (reduce each top number by 1 and multiply by 3).

40 18 (subtract 7 from each top number and multiply by 18).

41 D (reduce the solid to a line and add a horizontal stroke).

42 A (keep the flag in the same position, but reverse the other items above the base line and change the colour of the spot).

43 B (remove the right-hand edge and add a mirror image of the remainder).

44 D (superimpose the figures and rotate them).

45   C (the two figures represent side views and top views of the same pair of objects. A lens surmounted by a right pyramid is the only figure which fits).

46   C (all the others contain smaller versions of themselves cut in half. C does not).

47   C (all the others contain quadrant sections of themselves in smaller size).

48   A (the sections of the others are equal pieces).

49   C (the others can be halved to produce equal pieces with a dot in each).

50   E (each figure has as an appendix a smaller version of itself, drawn upside-down. E's appendix is drawn right-side-up).

51   D (rotate the figure by one eighth each time).

52   B (add the figures in the first two columns to get those in the third).

53   A (looking across the rows tells us that black spots sum to become white, but spots of alternate colour cancel. Looking down the columns tells us that white spots add to become white).

54   D (the frown and the stipple shading appear twice in each row and column, the triangle appears once).

55   C (repeated lines cancel).

56   B

57   A

58   Nine fire stations. Here is one solution:

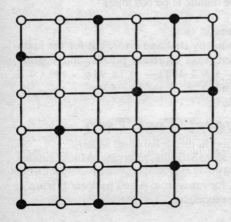

59   C (skip one letter on alternate tiles in each row).

60   A, B or E

61   TAX

62   GAME

63   BIN (robin, binary)

64   TAR (mortar, target)

65   INK (brink, inkling)

66   LIME (take the second and third letters in each word outside the brackets to form the word inside).

67   BACK (the fourth and second letters of the first word go with the first and third of the second word).

68   BALE (the fourth and first letter of the first word go with the fourth and first letter of the second).

69   PENGUIN (all the others are grazing farm animals: sheep, cow and horse).

70   CARPET (the others are table, chair and desk).

71   (b) (others *may* be true, but not necessarily so).

72   (b) £10

73   FOOTBALL, BACKSTROKE, EYELASH, GREEN FINGERS, SUN-HOUSE, ICELAND

74   2 (put three coins in each side. If equal, one of the other three must be underweight. If unequal, take two coins from the underweight pile and compare them. If equal, the last coin is underweight, if unequal, the lighter coin is at fault).

75   3

76   1,000 miles (i.e. one minute at 60,000 mph).

77   £24

78   No. There is the same in each.

79   £31.63 (it can be done by trial and error, but for the mathematically minded: let x represent pounds and y pence, then $100y + x - 5 = 2(100x + y)$, i.e. $98y - 199x = 5$. The only solution is $x = 31$ and $y = 63$).

80   10 (AD = BC = radius).

Answers: Test Two

1   J (skip alternate letters in the alphabetical series).

2   E (every third letter alphabetically, returning to the beginning when Z is reached).

3   Y (alternate letters, forwards from A and backwards from Z, in alternating sequences).

4 O and T (two series alternating, every sixth letter from B and C).

5 W (the interval between the letters increases by one each time).

6 J (backwards, the interval increases by one each time).

7 T (in the alphabet, the letters lie symmetrically about the first pair, M and N).

8 W (every seventh letter alphabetically).

9 E and P (two alternating series, one going backwards from H, one every second letter forwards from V).

10 P (every fifth letter backwards from J).

11 O or Y (alternate letters in sequence).

12 N (the sequences go from numerator to denominator; each
P alternate letter from F, and in increasing steps backwards from Z).

13 U (the interval between the letters is symmetrical about the central axis).

14 O (the interval between the top and bottom letters in each domino increases by 4, then 6, 8 and finally 10 steps).

15 S (an interval of three letters exists between each quadrant, going clockwise).

16 19 or 21 (two alternating series, going down in twos from 25 and 19, clockwise or upwards in twos from 19 anti-clockwise).

17 14 (the figure in the bottom cell is half the sum of the two above).

18 45 (the series increases by 6, then 8, 10 and finally 12).

19 17 and 20 (each step down is an addition of one, each step sideways an addition of two).

20 24 (numbers in the left-hand side of the circle are four times those in the corresponding right-hand segment).

21 21 (the numbers increase in steps of 2, 4, 8 and 16).

22 157 (the numbers decrease by 32 each time).

23 65 (each term is the addition of the two previous numbers).

24 $-1\frac{2}{3}$ (subtract $1\frac{1}{3}$ each time).

25 21 (each term is the sum of the previous two).

26 19 (there are two alternating series. The first is obtained by adding 3 to the squares of 1, 4, 7 and 10, the second by adding 3 to the squares of 7, 6, 5 and 4).

27 82 (the interval between each pair of numbers becomes the succeeding term in the series).

28 6 and 18 (two alternating series, increasing in twos from 12 and reducing in twos from 8).

29 18 (there are two alternating series, in each of which terms are doubled and the result reduced by 2 to form the next).

30 96 (the series increases by steps of 13, 15, 17 and 19).

31 U (the vowels go from numerator to denominator. Their
    6   position backwards from Z in the alphabet is opposite).

32 P (the numerical sequence is the squares of 1, 2, 3 and 4, and
    16   mark the position in the alphabet of the letters A, D, I and P).

33 H and 5 (the numbers in the dominos represent the position in the alphabet of the letters above).

34 C or W (every fourth letter in sequence).

35 R (alphabetical sequences below and above the horizontal).

36 C (the number of lines in the figure increases by 1 each time).

37 A (the lines and inner triangle move clockwise, and the outer triangle explodes away in alternate frames).

38 D (the shading moves clockwise, while the other figure traces the remaining edges).

39 D (figures with straight edges are shaded in the northwest and southeast quadrants, those with curved edges in the others).

40 C (the number of curved edges increases one by one).

41 7238 (the digits exchange places).

42 768 (multiply each term by 4 to get the next).

43 6 and 7 (two alternating series, one increasing, one decreasing).

44 67 (the numbers increase by 2, 4, 6, 16 and 32).

45 54 (divide by two and multiply by three alternately).

46 717 (there are two alternating series. One begins at 56 and is halved each time. The other begins at 87 and is formed by doubling the previous term and adding 3).

47 110 (begin with the series 1, 2, 3, 4, 5, 6; divide their cubes in half, and add 2).

48 22 (the interval is alternately 1 and 6).

49 26 (double each term and add 2 to get the next).

50 13 (two alternating series, one increasing by 6 each time, and one decreasing by 5).

51 8 (the terms on the bottom row are formed by taking half the product of those above it and subtracting 1).

52 7 and 24 (the top series progresses by $+1$, -2, $+3$ and -4; the bottom series by -1, $+2$, -3, $+4$).

53 6 (numbers on the left are three times those on the right).

54 40 (the series increases by 3, 4, 5, 6, 7, 8 and 9).

55 23 (the series go alternately from top to bottom. That start-
30 ing on 1 increases by 4, 5, 6 and 7; that from 4 by 5, 6, 7 and 8).

56 O (the top sequence is every third letter from C; the bottom
L is every third letter backwards from X).

57 7 (numbers in the top half are half those beneath them).

58 2 (the top row is the reverse of the bottom, with 1 added each time).

59 25 and 29 (steps across add 1 from left to right; steps down add 5).

60 L or A (skip 2 letters, then 3 to form the series).

61 X (the figures indicate the number of letters in the alpha-betical sequence between the previous term and the next one).

62 QP (there are two series, D, H, L, M with an interval of 4 letters each time, and K, M, O, Q with an interval of 2).

63 I E (there are two alternating series; each letter from A and each alternate letter from C).

64 E and R (the series go alternately from top to bottom. In each, one letter is skipped to get the next).

65 Q and M (each row has intervals of 2, 3, and 4 between the letters).

66 27 (the interval increases by 1 each time).

67 42 (each alternating series is reduced by 3 each time).

68 677 (square the previous term and add 1).

69 14 (there are two alternating series. One increases by 2, 3 and 4, the other decreases by 2, 3 and 4).

70 256 (take the squares of 0, 1, 2, 3 and 4, and multiply by 16).

71 14 (the interval between the terms increases by 1 each time).

72 225 (the series is 4 raised to the powers of 0, 1, 2, 3 and 4, minus 1).

73 357 (the series is 382 minus the squares of 1, 2, 3, 4 and 5).

74 101 (double the previous number and subtract 5).

75   65 (take the cubes of 1, 2, 3, 4 and add 1).

76   B (the vertical and horizontal lines, together with one of the diagonals, rotate clockwise. The other diagonal rotates anti-clockwise).

77   C (the number of dots in the figure equals the number of lines comprising the shape in the centre).

78   D (the two conjoined segments of the outer circle rotate clockwise, and the trailing segment colours the inner ring, which rotates anti-clockwise).

79   16 (in each line, the first term, plus the second and minus the third, is equal to the last).

80   130 (double each term and subtract 2 to find the next).

Answers: Test Three

1   B (the fish turn clockwise one quarter revolution in each row, or anti-clockwise one eighth revolution in each column).

2   D (the curved line rotates one quarter revolution clockwise in each row and anti-clockwise in each column. The straight line and dot are represented twice in each row and column).

3   B (in both rows and columns, black subtracts from black, while black adds to white).

4   A (the number of straight edges increases by one in each row).

5   E (the ball rotates round the triangles, which also rotate).

6   D (the third row is the sum of the first two, the third column similarly).

7   E (the ball rotates regularly, half of it remaining the same shade, the rest changing its shading from black through grey to white).

8   B (each different shape and different shading is represented once in each row or column).

9   B (the figure in the first column is formed by superimposing the other two and rotating them).

10   B (the hour hand moves forward two hours in each figure in the row, the minute hand moves forward 15, then 25, then 50 minutes).

11   D (repeated features cancel).

12   B (the lower line reduces as it moves right; the Xs on top grow in number as they move down).

13   A (in each row, shading on the same side of the vertical in the first two figures adds to form the third. Shading on opposite sides subtracts).

14   E (the second and third rows are cut from the figure directly above them in the first).

15   C (strokes above the line count as +1, those below count as −1).

16   E (the stippled area moves over each position; the other three kinds of shading are represented twice in each row and column).

17   C (dots add, but lines add only if repeated).

18   B (in each row there is one, two and three vertical lines, and one, two and three horizontals. Each different kind is represented in each row or column).

19   C (the first figure in each row is transformed as indicated by the second, to form the last).

20   C (striped skittles count as −1, plain as +1).

21   A (the striped area moves across, obscuring the shading underneath).

22   D (repeated squares cancel, repeated oblongs add).

23   A (repeated figures cancel).

24   C (the background shading increases from left to right. The ball stays in the same position, but the shadings add to black).

25   E (each upper and lower symbol appears only once in each row).

26   E (the pattern is formed from a circle, square or equilateral triangle, squeezed vertically or squashed horizontally, and changing its number).

27   C (the centre band remains the same, the outer bands get darker).

28   A (shadings add and are rotated).

29   A (lines are either straight, dotted or bent).

30   D (the figure explodes, although the cross-braces stretch).

31   C (the hatching pattern moves regularly down the figures).

32   B (the ball rotates anti-clockwise, the outer circle rotates clockwise).

33   A (similar shading adds; dissimilar shading cancels).

34 D (triangle, cross and circle rotate anti-clockwise; the inner dots occupy each corner of the triangle in turn).

35 E (white and black circles, white and black squares, white and black triangles all appear in groups of 1, 2 and 3 in the pattern).

36 C (in each row, the hour hand moves back regularly. The minute hand moves to where the hour hand was in the earlier figure).

37 E (in each row, outer dots count as +1, inner dots as −2. In each column, the same result occurs).

38 D (the shading moves progressively towards the centre in the sequence white, black, diagonal shading, horizontal shading, dots, white, etc.).

39 C (the square admits the background cross pattern, the white circle obscures it in each row).

40 A (the shading moves anti-clockwise, as does the circle. The dot moves clockwise in each row).

Answers: Test Four

1 F

2 2 and 3

3 12 squares, 24 triangles

4 Four wheels must be removed, thus (or symmetrically):

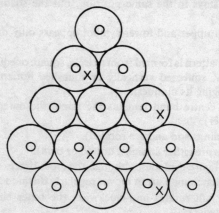

5   A HORSE, A HORSE, MY KINGDOM FOR A HORSE.

6

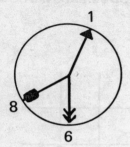

7   C

8

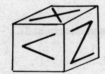

9

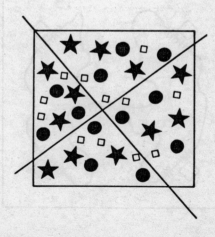

10   7,200 (80 rpm for 90 minutes).

11   1

12   YOU WILL FIND MANY GOOD FRIENDS IF YOU JOIN MENSA.

13   A

14   3 (i.e. $17 + 17 + 66$).

15   The only winning moves are:

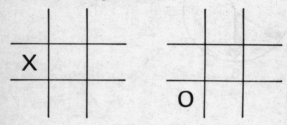

16   3

17   10 miles (vowels count 1, consonants count 2).

18   2 and 5

19   Two sets of points are needed, thus:

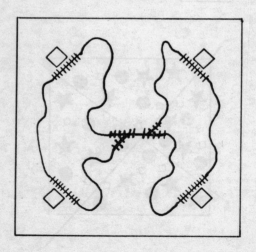

20

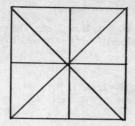

21 A, B and E

22 6¾ weeks

23 THE APPIAN WAY WAS A ROMAN ROAD (letters in alphabetical sequence start at A and work left to right, right to left up the grid).

24 16 routes

25 15

26 MARY HAD A LITTLE LAMB, ITS FLEECE WAS WHITE AS SNOW.

27 1 (take one sack from the first man, two from the second, and so on. Weigh them together. From the total shortfall can be calculated how many sacks are 5% light, and hence which man is the thief).

28 He says, 'If mine were white, B would see a white and a black and would deduce his own as black, because C does not go forward.' Since B has not made this deduction and claimed release, A knows his original assertion was wrong, and his must be black.

29 100 steps (downwards, the length is the 50 he walks plus x steps which disappear. Upwards, it is 125 minus the ½x steps which appear. Equating gives x = 50, i.e. 100 steps in all).

30 40 feet (open out the cuboid. The shortest path is the hypotenuse of a triangle whose other sides are 6 + 12 + 6 = 24 and 1 + 30 + 1 = 32).

31 Smith: English Literature and Physics; Jones: Chemistry and French; Browne: Car-mechanics and Maths.

32 50p

33 (d) and (e)

34 (c) and (e)

35 (b)

36 7.06

37 160 mph (take A = 1, B = 2, etc. Then multiply the first and last letter values).

38 24 plates

39 12p

40 96 (take A = 1, B = 2, etc.).